TALK TO ME

By
CHARACTER BUILDERS

Bonnie Sosé

Published by:

CHARACTER BUILDERS
Aloma Business Center
6922 Aloma Avenue
Winter Park, FL 32792
Tel. 407-677-7171
Fax 407-677-1010

Printed by:

VAUGHAN PRESS
823 W. Central Boulevard
Orlando, FL 32805

Cover Design - Bonnie Sosé

ISBN #0-9615279-7-8

DEDICATION

To my Lord, who is the constant source of my creative energy and ideas. To Richard, the man I love. To Bob and Rosalie, my parents, for their love, dedication, and constant support. To Holly, the light and love of my life. To Carl, the newest chapter in my life. **And to you, the reader.**

INTRODUCTION

People love to talk about themselves, so I have written a book that allows them to comfortably do so, while giving them, as well as you, the opportunity to ask questions that would normally be off limits.

How much time do you take to reflect about how you feel, what you believe, and how you live? When was the last time you tried to better understand those people in your world? Well, here is your chance.

Answer only those questions you feel comfortable with. Remember that you, as well as the people you share this book with, are entitled to privacy. Pass over the questions you feel are too personal to talk about and the questions that others seem reluctant to answer.

I hope this book proves to be a wonderful growth and learning experience for you. I know it has been for me. Good luck on your journey.

Love,

Bonnie

CONTENTS

IDEAS ON HOW TO USE THIS BOOK

- Evaluate important issues in your life

- Take on a weekend alone with your mate

- Use when entering a new relationship

- Use to reopen lines of communication with loved ones

- Choose fun questions to share at a social gathering with close friends or family

- Use as a learning tool for those contemplating marriage

- Use yourself, to see and understand yourself more clearly

- Share cherished childhood memories with your own children

- Write in answers to some of your favorite questions and send as a very personal gift

Consider giving as a gift for:

- Birthdays
- Valentine's Day
- Weddings or Showers
- Christmas
- Anniversary
- Mother's Day/Father's Day
- someone in the hospital

1. When was the last time someone loved you the way you needed to be loved?

2. If you were completely blind and could only see the heart of a person, do you think you would have chosen your present mate?

3. Go back to a time before you were married. What qualities made you fall in love with your mate? What made you choose your mate over someone else (give specific qualities)?

4. Can you recall the first home you shared with your mate? Share some special moments.

5. What is the most cherished memory you share with your mate?

6. Name seven specific things you really like about your mate.

7. When was the last time you:
   • took a moonlight walk together
   • listened to music together
   • cuddled on the couch
   • whistled at your mate
   • met for lunch?

8. What things do you need to hear more often from your mate?

9. What sparks your sexual passion? Does your mate's level of physical passion meet your needs? If no, what do you feel your mate could do to satisfy you on this level?

10. When it comes to your lovemaking, do you like it tough, tender, or a little of both?

11. What song would describe your relationship?

12. Can you tell your mate exactly what you need from him or her– your <u>real</u> wants and needs? What do you think your mate needs from you?

13. Do you like your mate to talk to you in bed? What words can spark your sexual appetite?

14. What sizes does your mate wear?
   - shoe
   - ring
   - shirt
   - dress
   - pants
   - hat
   - belt
   - nightgown or pajamas
   - underwear

15. In one sentence, describe your mate.

16. What is the strongest and most solid part of your relationship with your mate?

17. How spontaneous is your mate when it comes to lovemaking? How spontaneous are you?

18. If your success here on earth was based strictly on your ability to genuinely love – How successful would you consider yourself?

19. What kinds of things put you in a romantic mood? When was the last time you did something romantic with or for your mate?

20. You are happily married, but one day you innocently meet someone you consider to be your true soul partner. This person meets your every need and fulfills your every dream. What do you do?

21. In 20 words, describe your relationship or marriage.

22. When you are depressed or frustrated, can you rely on your mate for support? Can your mate rely on you?

23. Do both people in a marriage have equal responsibility concerning financial matters? How would you feel if your mate became ill and you were forced to become the sole support for your family?

24. Are there hobbies, common interests, or activities you share with your mate?

25. When was the last time you took a **steamy** shower with your mate?

26. When was the last time you had an intimate heart-to-heart talk with your mate?

27. When you are away from your mate, what are some of the simple things you miss?

28. What is the last thing you did to try to make your mate happy? Be specific.

29. When is the last time someone gave you the look of love?

30. Is there anything in your lovemaking that you haven't done that you would like to try?

31. What do you feel are the three main hindrances to true lasting love?

32. Does your mate have a good sense of humor? What about you? When was the last time you had a good laugh together? In what ways do you have a good time together?

33. Is your mate your best friend?

34. Where would you like to go and what would set the mood for a romantic vacation?

35. What do you bring to your relationship that makes it work?

36. You are late for work because you got caught up in a passionate lovemaking experience with your mate. Would you tell your boss the truth about why you are late?

37. Can you picture what your mate will look like in 20 years? What about you?

38. What did you find out about your mate **after** you married?

39. Are there times that you feel particularly close to your mate?

40. How much importance do you place on your mate's looks? What will be there when his/her looks are gone?

41. How much time do you spend with your mate each day? How often do you plan time to be alone together?

42. If your mate suddenly gained a great deal of weight, would it affect your relationship?

43. Is the way your mate kisses you important? How do you like to be kissed? When is the last time you had that kind of kiss?

44. How did you meet your mate? What was the first thing you noticed or were attracted to? What continues to attract you?

45. What is the best way for your mate to approach you after a fight?

46. Your mate wants to make you a special occasion meal. What would you want on the menu?

47. Have you ever been totally and completely in love?

48. Do you feel as one with your mate, heart, soul and mind?

49. What kinds of things did you do for your mate **before** you got married that you no longer take the time to do?

50. What would be the most difficult thing for you to deal with if your mate were to die today?

51. Are there any external pressures that affect your marriage?

52. Would you consider staying in a bad marriage for the sake of the children?

53. How soon after dating your mate did you consider a permanent relationship?

54. In what ways do you or can you depend on your mate?

55. If you are angry, does it affect your sex life?

56. How would you describe life with your mate?

57. Does your mate challenge you to grow?

58. Do you trust your mate completely? If no, where and at what point do you feel your trust has been broken?

59. Describe your sex life when you first got married. Describe your sex life now.

60. How do you feel when your mate is unresponsive to you sexually? How do you feel when your mate is in the mood for love and you're not?

61. Did you marry for love?

62. How do you greet your mate when you haven't seen him/her all day? How would you like your mate to greet you?

63. Do you like the sound of your mate's voice?

64. What is the key to success when it comes to finding love?

65. Can you recall the most romantic memories or experience you ever shared with someone?

66. You love your partner but there is no passion left in your relationship. How would you attempt to rekindle that fire?

67. How can you detect when your mate is upset? How do you usually respond to him/her at such times?

68. Would it affect your relationship if your mate had no interest in spiritual growth? What if anything do you share with your mate on this level?

69. Would you want to marry someone with your same qualities? Explain, why or why not?

70. Do you feel unconditionally loved by your mate, or do you feel he/she is always trying to change something about you?

71. Would you be happier in a calm, consistent relationship or a passionate, fire-filled, adventurous one?

72. In what ways is your mate unique?

73. What needs does your mate fulfill for you? Can you remember a time when your mate was particularly attentive to your needs?

74. How would you feel if your mate went out on a regular basis with single friends?

75. What kind of outdoor activities do you share with your mate?

76. Where and how did you or would you propose marriage?

77. Have you ever stayed in a relationship for all the wrong reasons? If yes, why did you stay?

78. When was the last time you:
    • tenderly kissed your mate
    • rented a motel room together
    • walked in the rain together
    • sang in the car together?
    • watched a sunrise or sunset together

79. What has caused most of the problems in your relationship with your mate?

80. Have you ever had a difficult time letting go of a relationship?

81. What would you do if you no longer felt physically attracted to your mate? How would you feel if your mate was no longer physically attracted to you?

82. Name something that you do strictly because it is important to your mate.

83. What should the penalty be for spouse abuse? What would you do if your mate abused you? Have you ever been abused in the past?

84. What do you find sexually attractive about your mate?

85. Is it easy for you to communicate your sexual needs in bed?

86. Do you and your mate have similar or different backgrounds? If different, in what way does that difference work for or against your relationship?

87. How much affection do you need? In what specific ways do you like your mate to show you affection? Are there certain times that you need more affection than other times?

88. What little things do you do for your mate? Would he/she do the same for you?

89. If your mate had bad debts from the past, would you feel any obligation if you were to marry?

90. When is the last time someone whispered sweet nothings in your ear?

91.   Has there ever been a time that you felt vulnerable to the temptation to have an affair?

92.   When was the last time you:
- complimented your mate
- saw a movie together
- really looked at your mate
- chased your mate around the house
- lovingly pinched or squeezed your mate?

93.   How can you distinguish between sexual attraction and real love?

94.   What is your routine upon going to bed? Upon waking up in the morning?

95.   Your mate loses a great deal of money in a failed business venture. This changes your lifestyle considerably. Will this affect your relationship?

96.   Are you sexually compatible with your mate?

97.   Have you ever had a secret love?

98. Are there specific things that keep the spark in your relationship? If yes, what?

99. Is love its own reward? Was there ever a time that you loved when your love was not returned?

100. How would you deal with a mate who was a complete mess around the house? What are some of the things you would like your mate to do around the house to help you?

101. Can you recall a time that you were fed up with your mate and considered ending your relationship?

102. What would you do if your mate suddenly started drinking or taking drugs?

103. Your mate can no longer engage in sexual activity due to illness. Would this change your relationship?

104. How important is spontaneity and creativity when it comes to making love? Can you recall the last time you did something that was unexpected and took some creativity on your part?

105. Do you see a talent in your mate that is undeveloped?

106. Your mate has lost his/her direction and drive in life. How could you help him/her get back on track?

107. Is it true that opposites attract? In what ways are you and your mate distinctly different? How do these differences work for or against your relationship?

108. When was the last time you made mad, passionate love?

109. Your doctor surprises you with the news that you're going to have a baby. Would this be good or bad news? How would this change your life?

110. What is the **one** key that would or did open your heart?

111. How and in what **specific ways** do you need your mate to show you attention and affection outside of lovemaking?

112. Do you have any sexual hang-ups or fears?

113. Who would you like to build a love nest with?

114. If you or your mate are out of shape does this affect your lovemaking?

115. What is the difference between being loving and acting loving? Can you recall experiencing such a distinction in your life?

116. When was the last time you:
    • undressed your mate for bed
    • bought something for your mate to wear to bed
    • gave your mate a private fashion show
    • were free-spirited in your lovemaking?

117. What does the word "helpmate" mean in a relationship?

118. When did your mate last surprise you? When did you last surprise your mate?

119. How romantic is your mate? How and in what ways are **you** romantic? Share your most romantic moment together.

120. Do you have a pet name for your mate? Does your mate have one for you? What affectionate words do you like to hear from your mate?

121. What is the ideal weather for lovemaking?

122. List five things that promote oneness in your marriage or relationship.

123. Has a friend of yours ever moved in on your relationship with your mate when you were having problems?

124. Have you ever received poetry from someone? Have you ever sent poetry to someone?

125. Have you ever taken a cruise with your mate? Where have you gone on vacation together?

126. In what ways do you help build your mate's self-esteem? In what ways do you tear it down?

127. How would you feel about your mate watching sports all weekend?

128. Do you like to sleep close to your mate or separately?

129. When did you know you had fallen in love?

130. How do you feel when you are ignored by your mate?

131. Would it bother you if your mate frequently had to leave town on business?

132. What do you feel you deserve from your mate?

133. If your mate wanted to end your relationship or marriage, how would you respond?

134. In what one area does your mate neglect you or your feelings?

135. When did you know that the honeymoon was over?

136. What did you do or where did you go the night before your wedding?

137. What have you learned from past relationships?

138. Do you want children? If so, how many? How would you feel if you found out you could never have children? What if you knew you would never marry?

139. Would you ever marry someone that your family totally disapproved of?

140. What sacrifices have you been willing to make for your mate? To what **extent** would you be willing to sacrifice for your mate?

141. Can you love someone that you cannot respect? Do you respect your mate? Does your mate treat you with respect? If yes, in what way?

142. Have you ever been in love with the idea of being in love?

143. Do you believe in divorce? Why do you feel there are so many divorces today? Is there anything your mate could do that would cause you to consider getting a divorce?

144. Are there certain areas of your life that you feel your mate has never really made the effort to completely understand?

145. Do you resent your mate when he/she nags you or gives you advice?

146. Would you ever consider going into business with your mate?

147. When was the last time you:
    • asked your mate to take you to bed
    • towel dried your mate after a shower
    • shared candlelight and wine
    • held each other?

148. Is there such a thing as love at first sight?

149. In what ways are you compatible with your mate?

150. On weekends, what do you do when you wake up and your mate is still sleeping?

151. Define the word "fidelity" as you see and understand it. How would you feel and what would you do if you found out your mate was unfaithful? What would your mate do if he/she found out you were unfaithful?

152. When was the last time you:
    • sent your mate a card
    • gave your mate a small gift
    • left a love note
    • sent a love letter
    • just called to say "I love you"?

153. What was your wedding like? Describe where it was held, type of ceremony, number of people attending, type of reception, and your overall feelings about this event. Who caught the bouquet?

154. Would you ever trade love for security? Have you ever stayed in a relationship for security?

155. Is love blind? Have you ever been blind in a relationship?

156. What would you do if your mate refused to work?

157. What common values do you share with your mate?

158. Do you affectionately share a song with your mate? What is your favorite love song?

159. Have you ever had your heart broken? Do you feel you have ever hurt someone else deeply?

160. How important is it to you that your mate is physically fit?

161. Do you share any creative interests with your mate?

162. What is the reality of your relationship?

163. When it comes to finding love, are you usually led by your heart or head?

164. How well do you and your mate communicate? Are there certain areas or certain subjects you have a difficult time communicating about with your mate? If yes, what?

165. Has your sex life ever been affected by the birth of a child?

166. Have you ever been in a relationship that was destructive?

167. If your partner expressed a desire for you to change your style of dress or hair, would you? How do you feel about your mate's grooming?

168. How often do you spend time with mutual friends? What common interests do you share with them? Which of your friends do you have the most fun with?

169. Do you ever feel that your mate takes you for granted? If yes, in what specific ways? Do you ever take your mate for granted?

170. Can you work on a project with your mate without bickering and arguing? What and when was the last time you worked on a project together?

171. How do you feel if your mate changes your plans at the last minute?

172. How do you feel about interracial marriage? Have you ever been involved in an interracial relationship?

173. Have you ever been involved in a love relationship where the love was stronger on one side? In such a case, would you rather be the one who loved more or the one who was loved? Is it a greater blessing to give or receive love?

174. Would you prefer to have an individual bank account or a joint account with your mate?

175. What would you consider mature, deep love?

176. Would you ever consider taking a vacation without your mate?

177. When have you felt emotionally neglected by your mate?

178. Women: Do you ever initiate lovemaking?

179.   Do you enjoy giving and receiving a body massage? When was the last time you gave your mate a body massage?

180.   How would you like your mate to respond to you after lovemaking?

181.   What kind of table manners does your mate have?

182.   Does your mate ever embarrass you in public? If yes, how did you respond?

183.   How do you flirt when you are attracted to someone?

184.   How would you feel about a long-distance relationship if the amount of money either you or your mate made was substantial?

185.   How do you feel about your mate's spending habits? If your mate complained about your spending too much money, how would you respond?

186. How has your mate influenced the way that you think, in either a positive or negative way?

187. What is the biggest difference between men and women?

188. What is the one habit you would like your mate to change?

189. How would you feel if you found out your mate lied to you? Do you lie to your mate?

190. Do you ever close your mate out? At what times would this most likely occur? What is the best way for your mate to respond to you at such times?

191. What is your fantasy about the ideal marriage? What would you consider unhealthy reasons for getting married?

192. What can you share with your mate about your family life and your years growing up that can help your mate understand you better?

193. When was the last time you:
- touched your mate's face or hair
- hugged each other
- gave your mate a manicure or pedicure
- took your mate somewhere special
- showed concern for your mate's feelings?

194. Can you and your mate agree to disagree, or does someone always have to win?

195. Your mate disappoints you. How will you respond? What kind of things would disappoint you?

196. Do you like to receive flowers? Do you have a favorite flower? When is the last time you received flowers or sent someone flowers?

197. Women - Are your moods affected by your menstrual cycle?

198. When someone insults your mate how do you respond?

199. Are there certain things you can brag about concerning your mate?

200. How do you feel when you are separated from your mate for a period of time? What is the longest period of time you feel comfortable being away from your mate?

201. Do you do something special for your mate on his/her birthday, or his/her anniversary?

202. How do you feel about your overall sex appeal?

203. What kind of underwear do you like your mate to wear? What do you like your mate to wear to bed?

204. What is the best and fairest way to end a relationship?

205. Have you ever been involved with someone who is considerably younger or older than you?

206. Where is the most unusual place you have ever made love?

207. What would be your ideal honeymoon? What do you remember about your honeymoon?

208. What is your most and least favorite social event to attend with your mate?

209. How much independence do you need?

210. Would you ever consider taking a candlelight bubble bath with your mate?

211. How can you keep love fresh?

212. How many times have you been married?

213. Do you have expectations in terms of your mate's earnings?

214. What does love feel like?

215. What expectations do you have concerning marriage?

216. What is the benefit of being married?

217. Describe a time in your relationship that things changed dramatically, either for the good or the bad.

218. Was there ever a time that you thought your marriage was over? What made you decide to try?

219. In what way do you make your mate feel valuable?

220. Describe the biggest fight you ever had with your mate.

221. How often do you and your mate cook together? What kinds of things do you talk about when you share a meal?

222. Is there someone you would like to meet? Where would be the best place for you to go to meet someone you might have something in common with? How would you let someone know if you were interested?

223. When is your anniversary? When is your mate's birthday?

224. When is the last time you had a conversation over the phone with your mate that put you in the mood for romance?

225. What is the most difficult problem you have worked through with your mate?

226. Have you ever played or has anyone ever played head games with you?

227. Does your mate criticize you? If yes, how has this affected you over the term of your relationship?

228. Would you feel threatened if your mate became more successful than you?

229. Do you have integrity? Do you think your mate has integrity?

230. When was the last time you:
     - had a real conversation with your mate
     - gave your mate an unexpected surprise
     - helped your mate around the house or with the kids
     - read to your mate
     - swam together?

231. If you couldn't stand your mate's best friend, what would you do or say?

232. If you had the opportunity to work in a distant city and have a learning experience that would change your life, but you would be separated from your mate for that entire period of time, what would you do?

233. How do you feel about oral sex?

234. If your mate were to die, would you be able to support yourself?

235. What is your idea of a real man? A real woman?

236. Tell your mate five things you admire about him/her.

237. What is the best way to get your mate out of a bad or depressed state of mind?

238. What would you do if you had an intense attraction to someone other than your mate?

239. What would you do if you realized that your relationship was in very serious trouble?

240. On a 1-10 scale, rate your relationship or marriage.

241. Your mate has just joined a new religion and has become very devout. How will you respond?

242. When is your favorite time for lovemaking and how often do you like to make love? What exactly do you like in bed?

243. What are the unwritten rules you live by in your relationship?

244. If your relationship has deteriorated, what specific incident or happening triggered this?

245. How much weight have you gained since the day you got married?

246. How can you tell when your mate is upset with you? How can your mate tell when you are upset with him/her?

247. Tell your mate something that's been bothering you for a long time.

248. When was the last time you:
- shared popcorn and a movie together
- bragged about your mate
- sent, gave, or picked your mate flowers
- ticked your mate's back
- winked at your mate?

249. Is the person you married the person you thought you married?

250. How would you feel if, after you married, you found out that your mate had been a nude dancer at a local sleazy club? What if they had been a drug addict, alcoholic, or prostitute?

251. What would you do if your mate brought home a venereal disease?

252. How would you feel if you realized someone else was very attracted to your mate?

253. Do you feel it's wrong to show your mate affection in public? Do you feel embarrassed if your mate shows you affection in public?

254. How would you feel if your mate was flirting with someone of the opposite sex?

255. How different would your life be today if you had not married your mate? What would your life be like if you had remained single?

256. Tell your mate the kind of gift you would like to receive from him/her on a special occasion.

257. Name one bad habit that your mate has that drives you out of your mind.

258. How do you let your mate know when you are in the mood for love? How does your mate let you know?

259. If your mate insulted you in front of friends, what would you say or do? Have you ever insulted your mate in front of other people?

260. Can love die? If there were no longer any love left in your relationship, what would you do?

261. What would you do if you felt you were outgrowing your mate? What if your mate was outgrowing you?

262. When is the last time you walked hand in hand along the beach with your mate?

263. Do you feel that your mate really **listens** and **hears** what you feel?

264. When is the last time you went away **alone** with your mate?

265. When you argue, do you ever try to see things from your mate's point of view?

266. What are some of the small things your mate does that helps you or makes you happy? What are some small things you would appreciate your mate doing?

267. Were there any behaviors you saw in your mate **before** you married that you thought might be a potential problem?

268. Have you ever chosen a person for the packaging rather than the contents?

269. If you were previously married, for what reasons do you think your marriage failed? Why does your ex-mate believe your marriage failed? How many times have you been married?

270. Have you ever been relationship-addicted? Do you ever feel lost when you're not involved with someone?

271. If you had to choose between the two, would you rather choose a mate who could supply your every "material" need or live in an old beat-up trailer with someone that you loved?

272. When was the last time you took your mate out on a date? Where did you go and what did you do? How often do you plan something special to share with your mate?

273. How would you feel if your mate had to work a great deal of overtime, including almost every weekend?

274. Can you recall a time that you felt you were unfair to your mate? If yes, in what way?

275. Could you remain loyal if your mate was sentenced to 10 years in prison? You are not sure whether he/she is innocent.

276. What is the longest period of time you have gone without sex?

277. What would you do if you found out your mate was involved in something dishonest and deceitful?

278. How do you think it would affect your relationship if you were with your mate all the time?

279. Do you follow your heart or head when it come to finding a mate?

280. How would you respond if you found out that your mate had a brief affair several years ago? What about an affair that was more recent?

281. When was the last time you:
- slow danced together
- fell asleep in each other's arms
- bathed your mate or took a bath together
- washed, combed, or brushed your mate's hair
- felt thankful for your mate?

282. Would you marry your mate again if you had to do it all over again? Has your partner been a help or hinderance in your journey through life together?

283. What do you find more stimulating— predictable or unpredictable lovemaking?

284. Do you have any fears when it comes to making a commitment? If yes, what is the root of that fear?

285. Do you know anyone who appears to have an ideal love relationship?

286. Are there ever times that you want to be physically close to your mate but not sexual? What is a nonsexual way that your mate can show you affection? At what times are you most likely to feel this?

287. Is there anything deceptive or dishonest about your relationship with your mate?

288. When was the last time you were childlike and playful with your mate (e.g., wrestling, pillow fighting, chase and catch, etc.)?

289. Do you tell your mate what makes you happy or do you expect him/her to read your mind?

290. When was the last time you did something special on Valentine's Day for your mate? When was the last time you felt like someone's special Valentine? What would make Valentine's Day special for you?

291. Has your level of sexual energy been different throughout different times in your life? At what age did you feel you were at your sexual peak?

292. What kind of music do you like making love to?

293. When was the last time you:
    - made your mate something special to eat
    - kissed your mate at an unexpected time
    - took your mate lunch
    - said the words "I love you"?

294. What is the longest period of time you have gone between love relationships?

295. How often do you and when was the last time you held your mate's hand? How often do you walk hand-in-hand together?

296. If your wealth and beauty were based strictly on your inward qualities, how valuable and attractive would you be?

297. What sounds do you find very pleasurable?

298. How much thought do you give to the way you live your life? Would you live any differently if, when the clock struck midnight each night, you would have no guarantee to life the following day?

299. What hobby do you enjoy? At what age did you start this hobby? What originally sparked your interest?

300. What is your idea of a little piece of heaven?

301. What is something new and exciting that you've experienced lately?

302. What is the greatest driving force in your life?
- money
- sex
- achievement
- acceptance of others
- recognition
- security
- self-understanding
- the quest for truth and knowledge

303. What is your favorite way to relax?

304. What would you consider your strongest point? Your weakest point?

305. What kinds of things do you like to do on the weekend?

306. Do you trust your instincts? Can you recall a time that your instincts were right on target?

307. In what areas of your life are you **most** self-disciplined? Least self-disciplined?

308. In what subjects do you consider yourself very knowledgeable?

309. Do you pray? If yes, how often?

310. What have you attained that took a lot of hard work?

311. Do you consider yourself a judgmental person, or can you easily accept people for exactly who and what they are? How do you feel when you are the one being judged?

312. When did you last take the time to pamper **your own** emotional, spiritual, or physical needs?

313. Do you believe in a personal God? What are your spiritual beliefs?

314. How often and when do you most need solitude? Where is your favorite place to go when you need to restore your soul?

315. How do you think people would feel and respond towards you if your **every thought both past and present about them, your every action, and your motives** were **completely transparent?**

316. "What" motivates you to work your hardest?

317. Define intelligence. How do you feel about your own level of intelligence?

318. How do you feel about your height, weight, and general appearance? What would be your ideal height and weight?

319.   Do you feel insecure about any part of your body?

320.   In conflict, do you usually:
       • yield
       • withdraw
       • compromise
       • resolve things
       • need to win?

321.   Name one area in which your performance is above average.

322.   Do you feel spiritually connected and in tune with any particular person? If yes, who?

323.   Name ten things for which you feel grateful.

324.   Describe your ultimate dream. Now, if you had that dream, where would you go from there?

325.   What is your greatest temptation?

326.   What do you feel is your **greatest** achievement or accomplishment in life?

327. What things do you consider beautiful?

328. If you had an opportunity to return to school, what course of study would you pursue?

329. In what ways do you think you are unique?

330. If you could start your life over again, what would you do differently?

331. What makes you respect someone? Whom do you respect? Do you respect yourself? Why or why not?

332. What is one quality of yours that draws people to you?

333. To whom do you feel intellectually matched?

334. What types of books do you like to read? Do you have an all-time favorite book? When and what was the last book you read? Where is your favorite place to read? Who is your favorite author?

335. How can you hold on to truth in a world of deception and illusion?

336. Do you like yourself? What **specific** qualities do you like about yourself?

337. In what ways do you consider yourself creative? Is there anyone you feel you can share your creative interests and ideas with?

338. How many hours of sleep do you need each night? What kind of mood are you in and how do you relate to others when you first wake up? What is your general morning routine like? Do you have a favorite time of day? Why?

339. When things get tough, are you prone to flight or fight?

340. Do you manage your time well? What percent of your time each day is spent in the following areas:
    - Job
    - Family
    - Self
    - Recreation
    - Spiritual
    - Hobbies
    - Social
    - Rest

341. What strong personality traits do you have, positive or negative, and how does it affect others?

342. What is the main area of your life that causes the greatest amount of stress for you? How do you deal with stress? What best helps you relieve stress?

343. Is it easy for you to share with others? Can you recall a time that you were selfish or greedy? Why do you think you responded the way you did?

344. How often and when are you most likely to feel lonely?

345. What arouses your curiosity? Name a curiosity that has never been satisfied.

346. What do you do strictly for pleasure?

347. At what time do you feel most attractive? Least attractive? What do you consider your best physical feature? What about your worst?

348. If you could be as free as a butterfly, what would you do?

349. What wisdom have you learned from life that you feel is valuable enough to pass on?

350. How will you deal with the physical changes in your appearance that come with age? How would you like to spend your golden years? Do you fear getting older? Visualize yourself at 75 years of age. How do you see yourself?

351. Share your tender side. What things can easily bring you to tears?

352. What is your greatest talent? Do you feel you have any untapped talents?

353. In what ways are you spontaneous and passionate about the way you live?

354. What is the most embarrassing thing that **could** happen to you? What is the most embarrassing thing that **has** happened to you? Is there anything that you have ever done that you are embarrassed about?

355. Assume you have enough to eat, have adequate shelter, and are free from illness. What then would be your next two greatest needs?

356. How important is it to you to continue learning? When is the last time you took a course or attended a seminar?

357. Do you read the Bible or some other type of spiritual material? If yes, how often?

358. Are you an optimist or a pessimist?

359. How different do you think your life will be one year from today? If you could, would you like to take a peek at your future?

360. When do you find it difficult to control your tongue? When have you said something that you later regretted?

361. Do you believe you have a guardian angel?

362. What kind of clothing do you feel most comfortable wearing?

363. Are you a type A or type B personality?

364. Who or what fills you when you feel empty or drained??

365.   Who do you think would be happy
        to see you become successful and
        who do you think would really rather
        see you fail?

366.   Have you ever been afraid to try
        because you thought you might fail?

367.   Do you hold a grudge? Has there
        ever been a time in your life that you
        sought revenge?

368.   Do you consider yourself a hard-
        working, conscientious person?
        When was the last time you gave
        100% at your job?

369.   How important is outside recognition
        and approval to you?

370.   What do you want out of life?

371.   What makes you happy? **Be specific.**

372.   Are you a day or night person?

373.   Are you liberal or conservative in
        your thinking?

374. Have you ever fallen into a lifestyle of mediocrity? What do you think caused this to happen?

375. If you were to die today, would you feel that you had really lived your life to the fullest?

376. What visual sights do you find very pleasurable?

377. What one thing would you consider a priceless treasure?

378. What would be the greatest news you could receive?

379. Define authenticity. How authentic do you really think you are? What about your life is **real** and what are the **false illusions** that you create for the rest of the world to see?

380. Would you consider plastic surgery if you wanted to change something about your physical appearance?

381. What are your biggest pet peeves?

382. What is your greatest weakness when it comes to food?

383. Who or what makes your knees go weak?

384. Is it possible to find the will of God for your personal life?

385. How do you act or react when you are upset? What kinds of things can easily upset you?

386. Who or what is the most important thing in your life?

387. What would be your favorite gift to receive from someone else?

388. What circumstances in life have caused you to turn out the way you are?

389. Have you ever been discriminated against? If yes, in what way?

390. Would you have the courage to start over again if you lost everything you owned in a major disaster? Where would you start?

391. What is the one thing that would be worse than death to you?

392. What is something you have always wanted to do but have never had the opportunity to do?

393. What makes you lose your temper? When was the last time you really lost your temper, and what caused it? What is the most outrageous thing you have ever done in a fit of anger? What were the circumstances around your rage? What is the best way for you to let off steam when you are angry? Is there a particular anger that keeps coming to the surface?

394. When the year 2000 rolls around, where do you think you'll be? What changes do you think will have taken place in your life?

395. When do you need privacy?

396. How do you entertain yourself?

397. What is something you could enjoy doing all day long? When is the last time you took the time for this?

398. What would you do if you discovered that you had a terminal illness and had two months to live?

399. Are there areas of your personality that you would like to change?

400. What does it take to whet your appetite and spark your drive to move forward?

401. What smells do you find very pleasurable?

402. What qualities do you have that make you lovable?

403. Whom or what do you find irresistible?

404. When did you last take the time to clean the **garbage** out of your mind and life? What kinds of things do you consider **mental** garbage?

405. Where is your favorite place to sing? How often do you sing? What kind of voice do you have?

406. Is your ability to give and take equally balanced? Would you consider yourself a taker or a giver? Explain why in either case.

407. Complete the sentence: I am a little selfish when it comes to . . .

408. When has your foolishness or selfishness hurt or damaged someone else's well-being?

409. How heavily do you rely on your intuition when it comes to making decisions?

410. At what age did you discover that you were a free-thinking individual entitled to your own feelings, thoughts, and ideas?

411. When did you have to let go of something that you weren't ready to let go of? When were you able to let go of the old and let in the new?

412. How much have you grown in the last ten years?

413. If you could return to any age and start all over again, what age would that be? What would you have done differently?

414. Most of us grow up with a lot of false information and negative programming. What ideas, values, and beliefs have you kept for your own, and what information have you thrown to the wind as false?

415. What brings out the child in you?

416. When you've done a good job, how do you usually reward yourself?

417. Complete this sentence: I am ready to fight when . . .

418. Who or what makes you feel intimidated? Why?

419. Who or what can make your heart turn soft?

420. How do you feel about your level of knowledge? Do you have a natural desire to increase your knowledge? In what ways do you pursue knowledge?

421. What is the most difficult emotional or mental pain you have ever had to deal with? What is the most difficult physical pain you have ever had to deal with?

422. At what times and in what situations do you feel most insecure? Can you recall the last time you felt this way?

423. Where and what do you see yourself doing five years from now? What were you doing five years ago?

424. What bad habits do you have?

425. Who or what really irritates you?

426. If you lost all your money and possessions, whom and what would you still have?

427. Has anyone ever physically abused you? If yes, who, when, in what way, and to what extent? Did the authorities ever get involved? What is your relationship with that person or those persons now?

428. What is your **greatest** fear? How would you react if this fear became a reality?

429. When did you pursue something that turned out to be a hollow illusion?

430. What do you normally do when you first arrive home from work? How do you greet your family?

431. How do you feel about your level of education? What was the level of education of your siblings, parents, grandparents, and great grandparents?

432. Are you a risk taker or do you play it safe? Can you recall the last time you took a **real** risk? What was the outcome?

433. Are you innovative? If yes, in what specific ways?

434. When was the last time you cried by yourself? When was the last time you cried in front of someone else? What made you cry?

435. Do you imitate others or do you try to be a true individual?

436. Do you play any musical instruments? Is there a musical instrument you would like to learn? Are there any people in your family who play musical instruments?

437. When is the last time you did something with a sense of flair and fantasy?

438. Do you vote? Who were the last three presidents you voted for?

439. How competitive are you? In what areas are you most competitive? Is there any particular person you regularly compete with?

440. What do you consider the biggest problem in your life?

441. Share a story about a time you had to speak in front of an audience. How do you feel about speaking in front of people?

442. Have you ever felt that you didn't quite measure up to someone else's expectations? Why do you think that this person's particular opinion carried such weight with you?

443. When is the last time you can remember feeling completely burned out?

444. When do you feel most energetic and alive?

445. Are you a leader or a follower? In what ways do you lead or follow?

446. What do you consider a daily struggle?

447. Describe a time when you needed help or felt helpless. Would it be difficult for you to ask for help if you needed it? Whom would you feel most comfortable going to at such a time?

448.   Do you have common sense?

449.   Whom can you go to when you need comfort?

450.   What nationality are you?

451.   Have you ever been angry enough to hurt someone? Have you ever been afraid that someone might hurt you? If yes, who and for what reason?

452.   If you gave your **everything**, what do you think you would really be capable of accomplishing?

453.   Do you consider yourself a generous person? When are you most generous and whom is it towards?

454.   Whom could you call if you were afraid? When have you been afraid? Are there certain things you are afraid of?

455.   What times and what kinds of things make you feel pressured? How do you function under pressure?

456. What do you consider valuable?

457. Do you like who you see in the mirror?

458. In what ways, if any, do you consider yourself wise?

459. Do you ever exaggerate when you tell a story?

460. In what outside activities do you enjoy participating?

461. What would you be willing to exchange for completely restored youth and health?

462. Do you plan things out or act spontaneously?

463. What do you spend your spare time doing?

464. Who or what makes you defensive? Why?

465. What do you need to make you feel secure?

466. What do you like to do on rainy days?

467. When is the last time you felt real joy?

468. When did you last listen and learn something?

469. How good is your memory?

470. Has there ever been a time in your life that you were dependent on another person? If yes, how did that make you feel?

471. What is your main purpose in life?

472. Is there a particular social setting that makes you feel insecure?

473. What goals have you set and achieved?

474. Do you believe that each soul has a purpose or mission? If yes, what do you think yours is?

475. How do you feel about going to a movie, a restaurant, or a party alone?

476. What would be your favorite city and state to live in?

477. What is your favorite climate to live in?

478. How often do you read the newspaper? What part of the newspaper do you enjoy reading first?

479. Would you consider yourself an original thinker? If yes, what was your last original thought? Whom do you know that you consider an original thinker?

480. At what times are you most likely to be lazy and unmotivated?

481. Do you feel guilty about anything?

482. How often do you smile?

483. How regularly do you give your opinion when it isn't solicited?

484. Is there any area of your life about which you feel great passion (work, hobby, relationship, etc.)?

485. What is the greatest truth about life that you have come to understand?

486. Do you keep a diary or journal? How would you feel if someone were to read it?

487. Do you ever meditate? If yes, how often and where? In what way do you feel it helps you?

488. Have you ever had the desire to perform in front of a large audience? What would you be doing?

489. Does your life have meaning? Who or what gives it meaning?

490. In what areas do you feel confident?

491. What is the one subject you know absolutely nothing about?

492. When you die, how do you want your funeral handled? What do you think will be said about you at your service? And what do you want written on your tombstone?

493. What gives you the creeps?

494. Whom do you feel protective toward?

495. What makes you feel satisfied?

496. Are there times when you feel cold and aloof? Are there certain people or things that trigger these feelings?

497. To whom do you feel thankful?

498. What is the one thing that you've done that was completely out of character for you?

499. What is the worst thing you **could** ever go through? What is the worst thing you **have** gone through?

500. Is there a sport at which you excel? Is there any sport that you dreamed of excelling at but never pursued?

501. What time do you like to go to bed at night? What time do you usually get up in the morning?

502. What vision do you have for the future?

503. Are there standard routines in your life?

504. What are some of the simple things you enjoy?

505. Overall, how do you feel about the way you look? Have your looks helped or hindered you in life?

506. Have you ever been so depressed that you actually thought about suicide?

507. Have you ever lain awake in torment over a situation?

508. At what times do you feel most insecure or unsure of yourself?

509. What are your favorite colors? What colors do you look best in? What colors would you use in decorating your home?

510. Describe a situation that took "real guts" for you to get through.

511. What do you think about most of the time?

512. When was the last time you danced all night? What type of dancing do you most enjoy? Have you ever taken dancing lessons?

513. When were you able to conquer a major battle in your own mind? What was the battle?

514. What is a worthwhile way to spend your time?

515. Can you recall a time that you were physically violent? What were the circumstances around your rage?

516.   How attractive are you on the **inside**? If you were turned inside out, what would you look like?

517.   Is there something for which you have never forgiven yourself?

518.   Do you have any phobias?

519.   If you could have named yourself, what name would you have chosen? How do you feel about the name you were given? What are the stories your parents tell about why they named you what they did? Have you ever changed or considered changing your name? If so, why?

520.   In what ways are you either practical or impractical? Are you logical in your thinking?

521.   What is the one thing that can immediately put you in a bad mood?

522.   Of what or whom are you intolerant?

523.   Do you procrastinate? When and about what types of things?

524.   Would you consider yourself predictable or unpredictable?

525.   What skills do you have that help you in life?

526.   What kind of temperament or disposition do you have?

527.   In what ways do you use your gifts, talents, and abilities outside work?

528.   How concerned are you about your grooming?

529.   In general, how do you feel your life is going right now?

530.   Do you feel comfortable allowing people to see you in a completely natural state (no makeup, hair uncombed, very casual dress, etc.)?

531.   Do you ever get depressed during the holidays? If yes, when does your depression start and how long does it usually last?

532. Can you recall a time that you decided to fight back (mentally, emotionally, or physically)? What was the outcome?

533. When you are pushed to your limit how do you respond?

534. Has there ever been a time that you knew you needed to make a change but didn't have the courage to do so?

535. How impulsive are you?

536. Are you searching for anybody or anything? What would you do if you found whom or what you were looking for?

537. Is the world a better place because you're here? When your life is over, what, if any, contribution to life will you leave behind?

538. What is your favorite in each of the following food categories?
- meat
- vegetable
- fruit
- beverage
- fast food
- ice cream
- candy
- munchie
- dessert

539. Do you feel you express your talents in the greatest possible way? Name one talent you would like to possess.

540. What is your favorite program to watch on TV?

541. Are title, position, or material possessions important to you?

542. In what ways do you work through your problems? Would you consider yourself a good problem solver? Recall a time that you creatively solved a difficult problem.

543. What do you take pride in?

544. Are you prejudiced? If yes, can you recall when and why your prejudice began?

545. What is the most difficult decision you have ever had to make? Do you feel you made the right choice?

546. How organized are you?

547. What has been your greatest reward for energies spent?

548. How good are your survival instincts?

549. Have you ever had a drinking problem? Have you ever been involved in treatment? Is there a history of any drinking problems in your family? If yes, do you feel this has affected your life in any way?

550. Do you have the ability to create something from nothing? Can you recall a time that you were able to do this?

551. Do you consider yourself an introvert or extrovert?

552. Did you ever receive a scholarship?

553. Women: When did you last:
   • have a Pap smear?
   • have a mammogram?
   • have a physical exam?

554. Have you ever been involved in the using or selling of illegal drugs?

555. Have you ever lost hope? If yes, when and why?

556. Have you ever gone to jail or prison? If yes, why?

557. Has there ever been a time that you completely lost control (physically, mentally, or emotionally)?

558. Whom or what kinds of things do you worry about?

559. What do you love to daydream about?

560. What obstacles have you overcome in your lifetime?

561. Does the thought of death scare you? Do you believe there is life after death? If you could have your dream of what heaven would be like **for you**, what would that be? Who would be the first person from your past that you would want to see and be reunited with?

562. What is the one thing that remains a mystery to you?

563. How would you choose to die if you had that choice? Would you want to know the exact date and time of your death?

564. Have you ever felt powerless to change your life?

565. How sensitive are you to other people's feelings?

566. Have you ever felt the need to seek counseling? If yes, do you feel that it helped you?

567. Do you have certain talents or gifts that have lain dormant for a long time?

568. In what areas, if any, do you think your level of understanding is enlightened?

569. What makes you sad?

570. Where is your favorite place to take a walk? Do you enjoy walking alone or with someone else?

571. How much and what kind of jewelry do you like to wear?

572. What is usually the last thing you think about before you go to sleep at night? What is the first thing you think about when you wake up in the morning?

573. What was the most beautiful rainbow you can ever remember seeing? What lies on the other side of **your** rainbow?

574. If you suddenly had to deal with a major handicap—like losing your arms—how would you cope?

575. What are your views on abortion? How do you feel in cases where the woman is a victim of rape?

576. Have you ever lived under a false illusion? In a state of denial? If yes, explain.

577. Name a situation where you feel you have "paid your dues."

578. Do you finish what you start? What is something you have left unfinished?

579. What was the most worthwhile thing you did today? What is the most worthwhile thing you have accomplished in the past year?

580.   Have you ever overcome any kind of addiction?

581.   How is your mental health? In general, how do you feel about your mind?

582.   How many times do you eat a day? What is your largest meal of the day? Where do you usually eat and whom do you usually eat with?

583.   How is your physical health? Do you exercise? How often and what types of exercise?

584.   Do you have any physical scars?

585.   What has been your most difficult physical challenge?

586.   What position do you sleep in at night? Are you a light or sound sleeper?

587.   Do you ever have a difficult time controlling what and how much you eat?

588. Have you ever been bitten or stung badly by anything?

589. Can you recall a time that you felt unstable?

590. How sensitive are you about your weight?

591. Do you ever fast? How often and for what reasons?

592. Are there any medications that you take on a regular basis?

593. Do you have any allergies?

594. Do you read food labels? How healthy are your eating habits?

595. How would it alter your life if you suddenly lost your eyesight?

596. What medical problems do you have?

597. Did you have any serious accidents as a young child? Have you ever been involved in a serious accident as an adult?

598. What is your blood type?

599. Have you ever delayed going to the doctor because of your fear of what he/she might find?

600. How is your emotional health?

601. Have you ever had a major or life-threatening illness?

602. Have you ever feared going insane?

603. Could you love a stepchild as much as you love your own? Would you treat a stepchild any differently than you would treat your own?

604. Has there ever been a time in your life that you felt there was a hole inside your soul that nothing could fill? What finally filled that hole?

605. Have you ever had the disease to please? What is the root of this feeling?

606. Have your motives ever been insincere? Has your insincerity ever backfired on you?

607. Has there ever been a time in your life that you were a rebel? If yes, in what ways did you rebel?

608. What is your birthstone?

609. How do you like to spend Sundays?

610. How many hours a day are you productive? How many hours a day do you waste? How could you rearrange your day in order to allow more time to do the things you really enjoy?

611. When have you felt like you were trapped and unable to do what you really wanted to do? Was your trap self-made or imposed from the outside?

612. Can you have a good time by yourself? If yes, what kinds of things do you do? At what times do you most like to be alone? How much time would you like to have each week just for yourself?

613. Are you frank and truthful with other people about how you feel?

614. When did you give up a piece of yourself?

615. How well do you adapt to change (major move, job change, illness, divorce, etc.)?

616. Can you tell a story about the most **irresponsible** period of time in your life? What age were you and in what ways did you consider yourself irresponsible?

617. At what age in your life did you feel most attractive physically?

618. Do you have trouble making decisions? If yes, over what types of things?

619. Do you like to live on the edge? Are you ever attracted to danger?

620. In one sentence, describe yourself. Now, in one sentence, describe how you think other people see you.

621. When are you most aggressive?

622. Can you recall the last time you asked for advice—what was it for, and **was it wise** advice?

623. If you were president of the United States, what changes would you make?

624. Give the sum total of all your life experiences as a **song title**.

625. What would you consider your favorite art form?

626. If you could ask God any question, what would that be? If He could ask you any one question, what do you think it would be?

627. Do you have a favorite saying?

628. How do you usually act at parties?

629. What is the one habit you can't seem to break?

630. What **one** person can you strongly identify with?

631. Have you ever taken part in a demonstration? If so, what and when?

632. When is the last time you let someone put you down and get away with it? Why do you think you let that person get away with it?

633. Has depression ever affected the manageability of your life? How long did your depression last and what finally brought you out of it? What kind of things trigger depression in you?

634. What is your most prized material possession?

635. Is there anyone that you feel dislikes you? If yes, why do you think they feel that way?

636. What kind of dinner do you prepare when you eat by yourself?

637. Name one thing that you do extremely well.

638. Everyone has a book inside him/her. What would your book be about?

639. In what areas do you consider yourself immature?

640. What do you usually wear to bed?

641. Name three material things you would like to own.

642. What is a major goal you have in life and how do you plan to achieve it?

643. Have you ever been brainwashed by anyone? If yes, by whom?

644. Write a convincing advertisement to sell yourself.

645. When Friday night rolls around, what do you usually want to do?

646. What food would you never be willing to eat?

647. Rate yourself as a 1-10 mentally, emotionally, physically, creatively, and spiritually.

648. Can you recall the greatest injustice you have ever experienced?

649. Can you recall a time when you were **able** to move past limitations you had set for yourself?

650. How do you personally distinguish between what you consider right and wrong?

651. What is the most personal or sentimental gift you have ever received from someone?

652. Are you devoted to any purpose or cause that is larger than yourself?

653. What is a subject that is very sensitive for you to talk about?

654. Life is a series of cycles; with each cycle our needs are different. What do you want or need at this stage in your life?

655. How good are your coping devices?

656. When have you had the guts to get your feet wet in a **different** stream?

657. When have you done something because of outside pressure or guilt instead of what you really wanted to do?

658. Who do you feel is an emotional support line for you?

659. On a 1-10 scale how would you rate your level of self-esteem?

660. How prepared would you be and what would you do if you faced:
   • Loss of your job
   • Loss of a mate
   • Loss of your health?

661. When was the last time you reflected on your life to decide if where you were going was **really** where you wanted to go?

662. Have you ever accepted a role assignment or label that restricted you or denied you the opportunity of expressing other dimensions of your personality? Were you ever able to pass through that invisible boundary? If yes, when?

663. What "shoulds" have you outgrown?

664. What self-defenses do you still carry around?

665. If you were to read a book about your own life, would you find it:
- interesting
- exciting
- boring
- a waste of your time
- in your opinion, a possible best seller?

666. What penalties have you paid for your unwillingness to risk change?

667. Is there a **personal mountain** that you want to make it to the top of? If yes, what's at the top of your mountain?

668. If you had been given a superior education, how different would your life have been?

669. Have you ever forfeited your own personal development to help someone else reach a dream? If yes, how do you feel about your decision to do so?

670. On a 1-10 scale, how would you rate yourself on an intimacy level? How easy is it for you to exchange your honest and true feelings with others?

671. Are you as concerned with your **inner** achievements as you are with your **outer** achievements? What do you feel you have achieved on an inner level?

672. Would you rather live a happy but shallow, simple life or struggle painfully and reach a level of deeper development?

673. If you could inherit someone's wisdom, knowledge, and understanding when he or she died, whose would that be?

674. How social are you? Do you find it easy to meet people and make friends? How often do you like to go out? Where do you like to go and what do you like to do?

675. What do you do when you cannot fall asleep?

676. Can you recall a time that you had gas at a very inappropriate time?

677. Have you ever hated anyone? If yes, why and what is your relationship with that person now?

678. When was the last time you laughed at yourself? Can you recall a time that you felt like people laughed at you?

679. Complete this sentence: I was not true to what I knew was right the time . . .

680. Is there any situation in which you felt that you lied or deceived yourself?

681. In what areas do you feel the most self-confident?

682. When have you felt most whole?

683. Has there ever been a time that you moved into a new and clearer level of understanding?

684. What activity is your most satisfying form of self-expression?

685. Is there anything in particular that acts as a stimulus for your creative energy?

686. Has there ever been someone's love that you wanted but couldn't or didn't have?

687. Have you ever been so totally absorbed in a creative process or work endeavor that it never occurred to you to compete, to compare yourself, or even care in the least concerning other people's opinion?

688. Describe yourself when you are at your worst and when you are at your best.

689. Have you ever felt misunderstood? If yes, when and in what way?

690. Do you gossip? How do you feel when you're around someone who shares negative information concerning someone else's life? When was the last time someone else's gossip hurt you? When did your gossip hurt someone else?

691. How caring, understanding, and respectful are you of the rights of others? Are you concerned about the dignity and well-being of all people?

692. Do you spend more time working on your public image or on your internal image? What do you have **inside** that no one can ever take from you?

693. Complete this sentence: I finally broke away and felt free the time I . . .

694. Whom can you talk **heart** to **heart** with?

695. What were your parents doing at your current age?

696. Would you have wanted someone like yourself as a parent? Why or why not?

697. Whose opinion carries a lot of weight with you?

698. Do you internalize anger or deal directly with situations and people? Has your anger ever led you to a physical confrontation?

699. Describe your family background.

700. Do you have the ability to separate the facts from the opinions of others and draw your own conclusions?

701. Who are the people who make you feel special? What specifically do they do that makes you feel this way?

702. What is the truest and deepest form of love that you have ever experienced?

703. How different were you from your own kids at their ages?

704. What kind of relationship do you have with your mother? What good or bad qualities did you inherit from her?

705. Who has hurt you most deeply in your life? Who has loved you most deeply in your life?

706. What kind of friend are you? What qualities do you look for in a friend? Who would you consider your best friend?

707. What kind of relationship do you have with your father? What good or bad qualities did you inherit from him?

708. Describe your mother. Do you like her as a person?

709. Describe your father. Do you like him as a person?

710. What do you feel that your parents taught you that has helped you become the person you are today?

711. If your parents had died when you were a young child, who would have raised you? Who would you have **wanted** to raise you?

712. What family member has had the greatest influence on your life?

713. Do you have any family recipes that have been passed down from generation to generation?

714. Whom do you admire and why? What personal qualities do you admire about yourself?

715. Name the one person you have the **most** fun with.

716. Have you ever interfered in someone's life and regretted it later?

717. Would you like to have someone similar to yourself as a friend?

718. What did your parents, grandparents, and great grandparents do for a living?

719. In what specific ways do you have fun with your children? When is the last time you had a good laugh together? What makes your children happy?

720. What are some of your favorite memories of your grandparents?

721. On occasion, your children will do something rare and wonderful. Can you recall such an incident? Are there any special moments you feel that you missed with your children?

722. What is the one thing that you wish your parents had done differently in raising you?

723. Can you recall a particularly difficult time you had relating to your father? What do you think was the cause of your problems?

724. Describe the personality and character of each one of your siblings. What kind of relationship do you have with them? What kind of relationship did you have with them when you were growing up? Would you have wanted them as friends if you were not related?

725. Do you have any stepparent stories to tell?

726. What is the one thing you have in common with your closest friend?

727. What is your **first** memory of your mother?

728. What was it like to visit your grandparents' home? How often did you visit?

729. When is the last time you went on a picnic with a lover, a friend, or your family? Where would be an ideal place for a picnic?

730. How and where did you meet your best friend?

731. What are some of the things your parents did **right**?

732. Whom do you feel uncomfortable around? Why? Whom do you feel very comfortable around? Why?

733. Describe a time or situation where you hurt someone verbally.

734. What things would have been left **unsaid** if you were to die today?

735. Who would you want to raise your young children if your life unexpectedly ended?

736. Who knows you better than anyone else?

737. If you could live in someone else's mind for a week and see life through that person's eyes, whom would you choose?

738. Can you recall a time that you had to let go of something or someone that you loved?

739. What is the most difficult thing you have ever had to forgive someone for?

740. What is the **one** thing you really hate to be nagged about?

741. Should household duties be equally shared? Who does what around your house?

742.	Do you know someone with a great sense of humor? How is your sense of humor and how much fun are you to be around? What kinds of things make you laugh?

743.	If you wrote a book about your family, what would the title be?

744.	Has there ever been something **profound** that happened in your life that caused you to change completely as a person?

745.	If you knew of a serious crime that someone in your family committed, would you turn him/her in?

746.	Have you ever been homesick? When and for what period of time?

747.	Would you know how to handle funeral arrangements if someone close to you died? Who would be the most difficult person for you to lose to death?

748.	Whom do you know who talks a lot but never really listens? How are your listening skills?

749. Do you feel you have any financial responsibility when it comes to helping an aging parent?

750. What is the best way to restore and heal an injured relationship? Are there any relationships you would like to try to heal? If yes, where would be the best place to start that process?

751. If you had no children or spouse, to whom would you leave your estate? Whom could you trust as executor of your will?

752. Who has the keys to your heart?

753. What are some things that you would change about your family life when you were growing up? What are some of the things you would **not** have wanted to change?

754. What makes a home **really** a home? Do you live in a house or a home?

755. Tell a story about your favorite Christmas or Hanukkah and your favorite Thanksgiving. Where were you and who did you share it with?

756. What is meal time like at your home? How often does everyone in your family sit down and share a meal together?

757. Was there someone besides your parents who gave you guidance as a child?

758. Have you ever had to deal with the death of someone you truly loved? How long did it take you to get through the grieving process?

759. Have you ever cared for someone throughout a prolonged illness?

760. What type of stepmother/father do you think you would make? Would you ever resent taking the responsibility for someone else's children?

761. Does your child have any natural talents?

762. Do you feel you measured up to your parents' expectations? What about your own expectations?

763. Do you ever feel guilty when you discipline your children? Have you ever felt that you disciplined them unfairly?

764. Is there someone that you feel great just being around. If yes, who and why?

765. What were your great grand- parents' first names? What do you know about them as people? How did they meet each other?

766. What kind of relationship do your children have with their grandparents? How often do your children see their grandparents?

767. What is the **first** memory you have of your father?

768. What time do you like to have your evening meal? What does your evening meal usually consist of? Is the way that food is prepared important to you?

769. Would you tell your sister if you knew her husband was cheating on her with her best friend?

770. Do you consider yourself loyal? Name the people to whom you have been most loyal. Who has been most loyal to you?

771. Who in your life would you like to develop a deeper relationship with?

772. Do you allow family or friends to influence your thinking and decision making when it pertains to your personal life?

773. Describe the **biggest** fight you ever had with your mother.

774. Describe the **biggest** fight you ever had with your father.

775. When you were home alone with your siblings, what usually went on?

776. Is there any unresolved anger that you feel towards any family member?

777. What do you feel is the most important thing you can teach your child?

778. If your child got into trouble, would you bail him/her out or allow the child to suffer the consequences of his/her actions?

779. A close relative comes for a visit and interferes with the way you run your home and the way you raise your children. Would you speak up?

780. What will you do and how will your life change when your children leave home?

781. Whom would you trust with a key to your house?

782. When is the last time you took special care in preparing a meal for your family or mate? When is the last time they prepared a special meal for you?

783. What good qualities do your kids have?

784. How affectionate were your parents towards you when you were a child? How affectionate were they towards each other?

785. Was your education important to you as a teenager? How important was it to your parents? Looking back, would you have handled your education any differently?

786. Were you ever jealous of a sibling? What was the jealousy over and how long did it last?

787. Did you ever have a physical confrontation with a parent? If yes, what was the outcome?

788. Whom could you stay with if you had no other place to go—no job, no money or food? Who could stay with you if they were in this situation?

789. Do you have any differences with your mate when it comes to raising your children?

790. Can you ever remember your father going through a painful time either emotionally or physically?

791. Name one significant contribution that you feel you have made to your family.

792. Do you feel valued by the people in your world? How many people actually exist in your own **personal world**? Give actual number and list the most important people in your world.

793. Name any childhood friends you still keep in contact with.

794. How would you deal with the death of one of your children?

795. Whom were you able to depend on when you were growing up? Whom can you depend on now?

796. How do you show your children physical affection?

797. Can you ever remember being made to feel small by someone? If yes, who?

798. Are you capable of being a supportive person? Can you recall a time that you were particularly supportive during someone else's crisis?

799. How is it possible to stay mentally and emotionally connected to a teenager? How connected are you or were you with your kids?

800. Is there a particular character trait that you like about either of your parents?

801. If your children spoke to you in a disrespectful manner, how would you handle it? What would you do if they became physically abusive towards you?

802. Can you recall a time when you really put your foot in your mouth? What was the outcome of your blunder?

803. Is there anyone you can be completely yourself around? Whom do you allow to see you at your absolute worst?

804. In what ways are you or were you a good example to your children?

805. When is the last time you told your father you loved him? What about your mother?

806. Are you proud of your children? If yes, why? Do you think they are proud of you?

807. Whom or what do you find refreshing?

808. Do you know anyone who is a true free spirit?

809. Whom do you love to hear from?

810. Whom do you feel most vulnerable towards when it comes to being totally honest about how you feel?

811. How do you feel when someone shows up at your door without calling first?

812. Do multiple births run in your family?

813. Do you like to barbecue with friends and family? When is the last time you had a barbecue with all the fixings?

814. How much power do you think that words actually have in terms of being a healing or destroying force? Describe a time when someone's words really hurt you.

815. Is there a history of any particular illness in your family?

816. Have you ever been in the position that you had to trust someone with your life? If you had to trust one person with your life, who would that person be?

817. What is the nicest unexpected thing you can ever remember someone doing for you?

818. How do you feel and respond when someone is always late? How often are you late?

819. Does it matter to you how your friends and family view your mate?

820. What type of religious training do you want for your children?

821. What did you try to give your kids?

822. When was the last time you roasted marshmallows or had a wiener roast with friends or family?

823. Do you feel bitter towards anyone?

824. In what **specific** ways do you show consideration for other people?

825. Have you ever wept over someone else's pain?

826. What is style? Whom do you know that has a sense of style?

827. When you die, whom would you want by your side?

828. When was the last time you took your kids to the zoo, a park, or to feed the ducks?

829. In what ways do you give love? **Be specific** (family, friends, and mate).

830. How often do you tell your children that you love them? How often do they tell you they love you? In what other ways do you show them affection?

831. Has your family ever gotten together for a family reunion? When, where, and what did you do?

832. In what way do you feel you influence people in your life in either a positive or negative manner?

833. Is there anyone to whom you would consider donating an organ in a life-and-death situation?

834. Have you ever felt used by someone? Have you ever used someone? What were the circumstances?

835. Do you have any particular qualities that make you or will make you a good parent?

836. Do you like to cook? What is your specialty when it comes to cooking or baking?

837. What chores do you dislike? What chores do you enjoy doing around the house? Do you feel everyone in your household does their fair share?

838. If your family wrote a biography about you, what would it reveal about you that the rest of the world doesn't know?

839. Do you feel that the communication was good between you and your parents when you were growing up? Why or why not?

840. What is one thing about your parents' relationship that you admired? Do you feel they were well-suited for one another?

841. In what ways do you or did you consider yourself a good mother or a good father?

842. How do you feel about the neighborhood you live in? How well do you know your neighbors? Have you had or do you have any problems with your neighbors?

843. How much freedom of individual expression were you allowed as a child? How much freedom do you allow your own children?

844. Are there members of your family who have drinking or drug problems? If yes, how has this affected you?

845. Who gives you unconditional love and acceptance? To whom do you give unconditional love and acceptance?

846. Have you ever done something that has benefitted the life of someone outside your immediate family?

847. Have you ever lost faith in yourself? Have you ever lost faith in someone else?

848. How would you like to decorate your home if money was not an issue? When is the last time you redecorated your home?

849. Do you have a favorite aunt, uncle, or cousin? Why do you think they are particularly special to you?

850. How patient are you with your children? How patient were your parents with you?

851. Tell a funny story about each one of your siblings.

852. What kinds of people are you drawn to?

853. How open are you when it comes to sharing your emotions?

854. When is the last time you dyed eggs or participated in an Easter Egg hunt with the children in your family?

855. Do you enjoy entertaining in your home? How often and what type of entertaining do you enjoy the most? Who are your favorite guests to have over?

856. Can you recall the first memory you have of each of your aunts, uncles, and cousins? What kind of relationship do you have with your relatives?

857. Have you ever had something stolen or mysteriously disappear from you or your home? What hunch or clues do you have concerning this situation and the whereabouts of what was taken?

858. Whom do you know that is full of life and enthusiastic about their approach to living?

859. What do you think that people's first impression of you is? What is the first thing you notice about someone when you are introduced?

860. Can you say NO easily to people when you really don't want to do something?

861. Would you ever consider helping your children get started in a business?

862. Have you ever planted a vegetable or herb garden? What would be your idea of the perfect garden? Do you enjoy gardening?

863. Could you go home to your family if you became unemployed or very ill? What family members could stay with you if they were ill?

864. Can you picture your parents as young lovers? How did your parents meet one another?

865. Have you ever designed and built a home from scratch? If you could design your dream house, what would it look like?

866. Is there anyone who has ever made you doubt your abilities? If yes, where are those people now and what are they doing with their own lives?

867. If one of your parents were having an affair, would you tell the other?

868. Is there a broken relationship in your life that could possibly be healed by a simple phone call or a couple of hours over lunch and a sincere desire to forgive and start over again?

869. Who can really get on your nerves?

870. What household projects would you like to take on this next year?

871. Is it easy for you to forgive someone? Are there people you have not forgiven? Are there people who have never forgiven you? If yes, for what reason?

872. Would you want to raise your children the way you were raised?

873. If it were possible would you want to know what people really thought about you?

874. How often do you give sincere affirmation to other people? How much affirmation do you need from other people?

875. Can you remember a time when you let someone down? Can you recall a time that someone let you down?

876. Do you reveal yourself to people, or do you project an image to please, provoke, or entice others?

877. How many times have you moved in your life? Where was your favorite place to live and why? Has a move ever affected you deeply in either a positive or negative manner?

878. When is the last time you had breakfast, lunch, or dinner with a close friend? Who is your favorite person to share a meal with?

879. Are you happy about how your children are turning out?

880. How do you respond when you are around critical, negative, or judgmental people?

881. If you are not married, what kind of wedding would you like? What kind of wedding would you like to give your daughter?

882. In what ways did you or do you consider your parents good parents?

883. What are some mistakes that you have made that you hope your children will avoid?

884. How would you have liked to raise a kid exactly like yourself?

885. What are some of the things you did as a teenager that your parents disagreed with?

886. What good points did you inherit from your parents?

887. Do you or did you read to your children? Did your parents read to you?

888. Did your mother stay home or work outside the home when you were a child?

889. How much personal attention did you get from your parents as a child?

890. When you were growing up, how were you treated by your relatives?

891. How do you deal with a closed-minded person?

892. How do you deal with rejection? Can you recall a time when you felt the pain of rejection?

893. How would you feel about older children returning home if they need financial help?

894. Has someone ever tried to control you? Have you ever tried to control the actions of other people?

895. How much compassion and empathy do you have for other people?

896. You find out that your son or daughter has loose morals. How will you handle this problem?

897. Is there anyone in your family or a friend that you constantly worry about?

898. Are your parents special? If you think so, how do you let them know that you think they are special?

899. How often do you go out on family outings? Where is your favorite place to go?

900. Are or were you a good provider for your family? Were your parents good providers for you?

901. Your best friend only has time for you when she/he is in between lovers. How do you deal with this?

902. Your 16-year-old daughter wants to date a 24-year-old man. What would you tell her?

903. Would you consent to your son or daughter getting married under age? How old were you when you got married?

904. Is there one particular thing that your child does that really upsets you?

905. A close family member is constantly beating his/her children. Would you report your relative to protective services?

906. Is there a friend you have lost contact with whom you really cared about? Would you be interested in locating this friend?

907. Were there favored children in your family? Is yes, who were they and why do you think they got special treatment? How did this affect your relationship with the people involved?

908. What would you do if your daughter's date showed up and was a different race?

909. How would you feel about caring for an elderly parent? What would you do if you lived in a distant city and a parent suddenly needed your full-time help? Would you ever consider putting him/her in a nursing home? Would you be willing to care for your parents in your own home if he/she needed constant supervision?

910. Your son comes home with a Mohawk haircut and an earring in his ear. How will you respond?

911. If you knew someone in your family was being molested by someone else in the family, would you report him/her?

912. What do you think your child would do if he/she got lost? What if someone tried to pick your child up while walking home from school?

913. What advice would you give your child if he/she were getting married?

914. What do you do when your child does a sloppy job on chores around the house?

915. What kind of table manners do your children have? What about your mate?

916. What is your child's favorite subject in school? What was your favorite subject in school?

917. What do you think your children worry about? What kinds of things did you worry about at this same age? What things do you worry about concerning your children?

918. Who is the most gentle-natured person you know?

919. Is there anyone you could rely on for financial help? Whom would you be willing to help financially if the need arose?

920. Is there anyone to whom you owe an apology?

921. How would you handle your child's unsatisfactory report card?

922. Can you remember being rocked or sung to as a child? If yes, by whom?

923. You see your children going down the wrong road. How would you try to turn them around?

924. In what areas are you particularly strict with your children? In what areas are you lenient?

925. Should a mother stay home and care for her children? What about a father?

926. What would you consider to be the ideal family life?

927. Do your kids ever embarrass you? Can you recall a specific instance? Have your children ever told you that they were embarrassed by something you did or said? If yes, what?

928. Has a friend ever saved your skin? If yes, what happened?

929. Your best friend's mate abuses her on a regular basis. She is unable to financially support herself. How would you counsel her?

930. When is your anniversary and how would you like to spend it?

931. Can you remember your mother going through a painful time emotionally or physically?

932. Would you ever consider taking a trip with a best friend instead of your mate?

933. How was sex education approached in your family? How did you or how will you approach sex education with your own children?

934. Is there anything your children could do that would cause you to disown them, or are you committed to them entirely, regardless of what happens?

935. Have you ever really helped a friend out of a tough situation?

936. What was your parents' reaction to your mate the first time they met?

937. When you're angry, what is the best way for someone to approach you in an attempt to re-open the lines of communication?

938. Do you ever act differently around different people? If yes, who and why?

939. Can you recall a kindness you did for someone that was 100% from the heart?

940. Is there any one person you felt had a detrimental effect on your life?

941. Have you been a bad example in any way for your kids?

942. What are some mistakes that your family made that you will not repeat?

943. Whom can you depend on? Who can depend on you?

944. How would you cope with being a single parent if something happened to your mate?

945. How do you feel or respond when someone fails to acknowledge you or completely ignores you?

946. How would you handle a mate, co-worker, or friend who had a hygiene problem?

947. If you were to lose everything you had, who would still be there for you? Could your friends and family depend on you if they lost everything they had?

948. Have you ever found anything in your parents' house that shocked you?

949. How deep is your capacity to love?

950. How do you feel about your in-laws? How do your in-laws feel about you?

951. What do you consider "interference" from your in-laws?

952. Should children have a say in planning family activities? When is the last time you did something they suggested?

953. When are your mother's and father's birthdays and when is their anniversary?

954. How do you respond when people tell you their problems?

955. Have you ever been taken advantage of by another person?

956. What are you most likely to do at a party or family get together? What was the most memorable time you shared with your entire family?

957. What is your reaction when someone puts you down?

958. How do you or would you deal with someone else's unruly children in your home?

959. Have you ever felt like a phony? If yes, when and in what way?

960. How happy are you in your present home? What made you choose to live there?

961. Who are the people who have helped you most on your journey through life?

962. Can you remember a specific relative going through a traumatic experience?

963. How do you like to be cared for when you are sick? How do you care for those around you when they are sick?

964. Can you see yourself as a grandparent? What about as a great grandparent?

965. What is class? Do you know anyone with this quality?

966. You find out that a dear friend or close family member has a drug problem. What do you do?

967. What is the most important thing you have taught your children?

968. Men - what kind of father were you or are you? What specifically did you or do you give your children?

969. How much respect do you give your children? How much respect do they give you?

970. How often do you or did you speak to your children in a harsh, critical, or demeaning manner?

971. Do you know anyone who is a little eccentric? If yes, in what way?

972. How clean and organized is your household?

973. What is the most creative gift you have ever given someone? What is the most creative gift someone has given you?

974. Whom do you know who hears and marches to the beat of a different drummer?

975. How do you feel about friends, relatives or guests staying in your home? How long are you comfortable with guests? Have you ever had to ask someone to leave your home? If yes, who and what were the circumstances?

976. Have you ever hurt someone emotionally or physically?

977. Is it easy for you to say "I'm sorry"? When was the last time you said those words and meant it? When was the last time you needed to hear those words?

978. Whom do you spend the most time talking to on the telephone?

979. When you give something or do something special for someone, do you expect something in return?

980. Is there anyone whom you treat better than your own family? If yes, who and why?

981. When was the last time you **really** listened to someone?

982. Does it bother you to be around someone who smokes? If yes, what do you say at such times? Do you or have you ever smoked? If yes, for how many years?

983. What was your birth order? How did it affect you?

984. Should single people be allowed to adopt children?

985. A close friend confides that he/she has contracted AIDS. Would this change your relationship? What would you do if a family member contracted AIDS?

986. What would you do if your son or daughter told you he or she was gay?

987. Can you keep a secret? When is the last time you betrayed a trust?

988. Is there something in your home that you treasure dearly?

989. Women - Have you ever experienced post-partum depression?

990. Who does most of the cooking in your home? Who cleans up?

991. If you could be invisible, whose life would you like to have a peek at?

992. Can you recall the first time someone sent you flowers? When was the last time you sent someone flowers? What would be your favorite type of flower to receive from someone?

993. When is the last time you shared a candlelight dinner with someone?

994. If every intimate detail, thought, and action including your deepest, most private secrets were exposed for the world to see, what would you do and how would you feel?

995. Do you allow or have you ever allowed other people to define who you are? When did you last have the smarts and courage to look within yourself and decide for yourself who you really were?

996. If the need arose, would you allow your mate's children from a previous marriage to live with you?

997. Whom would you not trust as far as you could throw? Whom could you trust with anything?

998. Have you ever been ashamed of where you lived?

999. What would you like to see your children do with their lives?

1000. What would you say if one of your kids walked into the room when you were making love?

1001. When you go out with your friends, where do you go and what do you usually do?

1002. What changes in your life could you make in order to have more time with your mate and family? How much time alone do you spend with your mate and your children?

1003. What is something funny, but also totally gross or disgusting that your mate or kids do?

1004. Can you make a statement praising your children?

1005. If you could vent your honest feelings about your in-laws, what names, if any, might you call them?

1006. What would be the most ideal family pet?

1007. You forbid your child to do something and your mate overrules you and tells the child it's okay. What would you do?

1008. What would you do if you found out that your child was a severe behavior problem in school?

1009. Have outside pursuits ever taken you away from family responsibility? How did this affect your family?

1010. Can you recall the most adorable thing you can ever remember your child doing?

1011. If you redecorated your home and then realized you hated it, would you live with it or change it?

1012. How do you select and what kind of gifts do you usually buy for your lover, friends, and family?

1013. What income do you plan to live on when you retire? Do you think your children should be willing to take care of you in your old age? Would you feel okay if an in-law or aging family member needed to live with you?

1014. If you were an adoptive parent, would you resent it if your child felt the need to seek out and establish a relationship with his/her biological parents?

1015. How would you feel if a child you had put up for adoption in your youth appeared on your doorstep and wanted a relationship with you?

1016. At what age did you break the dependence you had on your parents?

1017. When was the last time there were happy feelings coming from your kitchen or laughter at your dinner table? When was the last time you enjoyed the wonderful smell of something cooking in your home?

1018. What transitions have occurred in your family in the past five years? Which was the most difficult transition for you to handle?
- marriages or divorces
- illnesses or deaths
- major moves
- career changes

1019. When is the last time you stopped being a parent for a minute and tried to understand your kids - heart to heart?

1020. Are you thin-skinned and sensitive to criticism? When was the last time someone hurt your feelings?

1021. How easy or difficult is it for you to connect with other people?

1022. Tell a funny story about something one of your siblings did.

1023. What bonds of loyalty and trust do you cherish?

1024. What do you think is the biggest problem in the American family today?

1025. Has there ever been a family disagreement or misunderstanding that has put years of distance or noncommunication between family members? If yes, looking back, how could the situation have been handled differently?

1026. Have you ever been betrayed by a friend? Have you ever betrayed a friend? If yes, explain.

1027. What is the best investment you can make in your children?

1028. How are you like your mother? How about your father?

1029. Complete this sentence: The one person I can always count on to always encourage me is . . .

1030. Would you pull your child from an athletic team if his/her grades slipped? You realize that team involvement is important to your child's self-image.

1031. What do you think your parents' main goals in life were? How were their goals different from yours?

1032. What do you know about your parents' wedding day? Where did they go on their honeymoon?

1033. Is there anyone in your life who has remained your lifetime friend?

1034. Who has the #1 position in your life?

1035. How would you feel and what would you do if your child was born with some type of defect?

1036. Did you ever date someone your parents disapproved of? What would you do if you strongly disagreed with someone your teenage son or daughter were dating?

1037. What do you most enjoy about your home?

1038. What is your favorite way to spend your evenings at home?

1039. Can you count how many real friends you have? Who do you think would consider you a real friend?

1040. Did you ever go to camp as a youth? If yes, share your experience.

1041. What would you do if you walked into your teenage son's room and he was making love to his girlfriend? What if it was your daughter with her boyfriend?

1042. What are some of the fun or traditional things that go on at your house during Christmas or other religious holiday?

1043. Has anything happened in your life that you would consider a tragedy?

1044. What would you do if your teenager:
   • quit school?
   • became pregnant?
   • experimented with drugs?
   • was involved in satanic worship?
   • was dating someone you disliked?

1045. How much time do you spend alone with your children? Recall a special moment you shared together.

1046. Can you recall a time that you were really proud of your child? Brag a little.

1047. Is there an atmosphere of love in your home?

1048. Are there certain personal possessions you would like specific people to have when you die? If yes, which possessions would you leave to which specific persons?

1049. At what age did you get your **first** taste of freedom?

1050. If you could freeze a moment in time, what moment would that be?

1051. Tell a story about your **first** job. How old were you and what did you do? What kind of salary did you earn?

1052. Who was your closest childhood friend? Tell a story about your other childhood friendships, the **gang** you hung out with. Where are these friends now and what do you think they are doing with their lives?

1053. Describe a time in your life that you considered your **finest** hour.

1054. Share a funny story told by your family about when you were growing up.

1055. What is your **earliest** childhood memory? What is your most **treasured** childhood memory?

1056. What is the most adventurous thing you did as a youth? What about as an adult?

1057. What was the scariest experience you had as a child? What about in your adult years?

1058. Can you recall the most content period of your life? What made you feel that way?

1059. Can you remember a period of time that you had particular difficulty relating to your mother? What do you think was the cause of your problems?

1060. Describe how you saw yourself as a child and how you felt about your childhood years.

1061. Where did you live as a child? Describe your neighborhood and the home or homes you lived in. How many times did you move and which move affected you the most?

1062. Who were your favorite teachers throughout your school years? Tell why.

1063. Have you ever had a very **eerie** experience?

1064. At what age did you get your **first** car? What year, make and model was it? Who taught you to drive?

1065. What kind of teenager were you? What kind of relationship did you have with your parents? How would they have described you as a teenager?

1066. Can you describe your best and worst vacations? What would be your ideal vacation? When is the last time you took a real vacation? Where did you go and what did you do?

1067. When did you take your first train ride? How old were you and where did you go? Describe your most memorable train ride.

1068. Have you ever saved someone's life? How and when? Has someone ever saved your life?

1069. Tell your favorite camping trip story.

1070. When were you last surprised? When was the last time you had a surprise for someone else? What is the best surprise you could ever get?

1071. Have you ever stolen anything? If yes, what did you steal and who did you steal from? Did you get caught? If yes, what were the consequences of your actions?

1072. How did you celebrate your 21st birthday? What were you doing at that age, and what frame of mind were you in?

1073. What were you doing at age 25, and what frame of mind were you in?

1074. Did you collect anything as a child? What about as an adult?

1075. How did you make money as a teenager?

1076. In high school what should you have been voted the most likely to succeed at?

1077. Did you go through a period of rebellion as a teenager? In what ways did you act it out? What was the worst trouble you got into as a teenager?

1078. As a youth what was your favorite thing to do or place to go with a parent? What about with your friends?

1079. Women - Tell a story about the birth of each of your children. What was your first reaction when you found out you were pregnant? How did you feel about being pregnant at that particular point in your life? What were your term and delivery like?

1080. Can you recall a time that you gave in to peer pressure as a teenager?

1081. Who were your high school friends? What were they like, and what did you have in common? What do you think they are doing with their lives today? What is your fondest memory of your high school days?

1082. What were your childhood hopes and dreams about your future?

1083. Did you ever run away or consider running away as a child or teenager? If yes, where did you go, what did you do, and how long were you gone? What were the consequences when you returned home?

1084. As a child or teenager, did you play any particular sport well? Were you ever injured in a sporting event? How active were your parents in supporting your activities, and what other types of activities did you participate in at school?

1085. Can you remember a time that you cut class with friends in high school? Where did you go and what did you do?

1086. Who do you remember giving you the most tenderness as a child?

1087. Describe what you looked like as a teenager (age 13). What kind of attitude did you have?

1088. Tell a story about a time you missed curfew as a teenager. What was the outcome?

1089. Tell your worst bad weather story.

1090. How were you viewed by most of your teachers and classmates in elementary, junior high, and high school?

1091. Tell a story about your first **real** kiss. Now tell a story about your all-time best kiss.

1092. What is the most wonderful time that you can remember sharing with a childhood friend or friends?

1093. Describe your bedroom as a child and as a teenager.

1094. What is the first memory you have of doing something special with your mother?

1095. At what point in your life do you remember having the most intense emotional and mental growth?

1096. At what times in your life have you been a light for someone else's path?

1097. What is your first memory of each of your siblings? In general, how well did you get along with each other? How and in what ways has your relationship changed over the years?

1098. Can you remember a Christmas in your childhood that was particularly happy and one that was sad?

1099. At whose house besides your own did you spend a lot of time as a kid? Which of your friends spent a lot of time in your home?

1100. What was your high school graduation like? What did you do immediately after graduating from high school? What about college?

1101. Can you recall the most exciting thing that has ever happened to you?

1102. Tell a story about a prank that someone played on you as a kid or an adult. Now tell a story about a prank you played on someone else. Did you ever make prank phone calls as a kid?

1103. What is the first memory of your grandmother or grandfather? What were they like as people? What kind of relationship did you have with them? What, if anything, were they able to teach you about life?

1104. What was your worst report card story? What kind of student were you and what kind of grades did you get throughout school?

1105. What was meal time like in your home as a child? Who did most of the cooking? Did your family eat together? Was there anyone outside your family who was frequently invited to stay for dinner?

1106. Can you recall your most wonderful or interesting dream and your all-time worst nightmare? Have you ever had a recurring dream?

1107. Have you ever been embarrassed by someone or something that has happened in your family?

1108. Have you ever felt shame concerning any area of your life?

1109. Have you ever received a phone call that scared you?

1110. How well did you deal with turning 40 years old? What did you do on your 40th birthday? Were you happy with your life at that point? What were you doing at that age?

1111. What were you doing and what frame of mind were you in at age 30?

1112. What household responsibilities did you have as a teenager? Did you have any responsibilities you considered unusual as a youth?

1113. What were your favorite activities in junior high and high school? What, if any, clubs did you belong to?

1114. As a kid, how often did you sleep over at someone else's house? How often did you have someone spend the night at your house?

1115. Can you recall a particularly happy experience that you shared with a sibling when you were growing up?

1116. As a child what kinds of things did you do after school? What about on the weekends?

1117. At what age did you take your first drink or smoke your first cigarette? Did you ever have a confrontation with a parent over either of these issues?

1118. As a kid, did you ever sneak into a drive-in or movie theater without paying?

1119. Did you ever get into serious trouble as a teenager? What about as a young adult? If yes, what happened?

1120. Did you ever play one parent against the other as a youth?

1121. Tell a story about your **first** date. At what age were you first allowed to date?

1122. When you were growing up, who made most of the decisions in your family? Were you allowed to have your say when it came to decisions that concerned your life?

1123. How did your parents discipline you? What was the worst punishment you can remember? Did you ever feel that the discipline was unjust, misplaced, or too severe?

1124. How much supervision did you have as a child?

1125. Can you recall a time when your feelings were deeply hurt?

1126. Did you ever sneak out of the house as a kid or teenager? If yes, where did you go and what did you do? Did you get caught? If so, what were the consequences?

1127. Tell your worst flat tire or car trouble story.

1128. At what age did you learn to swim? Who taught you?

1129. Tell a story about the first time you left home for good. How old were you? Where did you go, and what did you do?

1130. What customs and traditions were practiced in your home when you were growing up? Do you practice any customs and traditions in your home now?

1131. Have you ever had a close encounter with death? Have you or do you know of anyone who has had a **near-death** experience? If yes, explain.

1132. Looking at the past, what is the one thing you would change if you could?

1133. Can you recall ever being stuck between a rock and a hard place?

1134. What kind of things can you recall doing as a family? How often did you do things together?

1135. Were you ever responsible for the care of younger brothers and sisters? If so, how did you feel about this?

1136. Did you come from a divorced family? If so, how did you deal with the break-up of your family? Looking back, **if you were given the same circumstances** as your parents, would you have made the same decision that they did?

1137. Can you recall a vacation that your family took together when you were growing up?

1138. Were you a stepchild? If yes, what was your relationship with your stepparent?

1139. What was your social life like in high school?

1140. When did you lose your innocence about life?

1141. When is the last time someone served you breakfast in bed? When was the last time you served someone breakfast in bed?

1142. Tell a story about a time that someone really messed up your hair (cut, color, perm, etc.).

1143. Tell a story about something interesting you found in the attic or some other secluded place.

1144. Tell a story about your favorite fishing trip. What was your all-time best catch?

1145. What is your first memory of each of your aunts? What about your first memory of each of your uncles?

1146. Describe your worst plumbing nightmare.

1147. Can you recall a time that you were scared by something you thought you heard in the middle of the night?

1148. Tell a story about your worst hotel/motel nightmare.

1149. At what age did you get your first bicycle? Who taught you to ride it?

1150. Is there anyone who devalued you as a child? If yes, who and in what way? What kind of relationship do you have with that person now?

1151. What fears and insecurities did you have as a child, teenager, and young adult?

1152. What was your worst disappointment as a child? As an adult?

1153. Can you remember a fist fight that you got into as a youth? What was the fight over and what was the outcome?

1154. Have you ever been horseback riding? When and with whom?

1155. When you were a teenager did you ever sample alcohol from your parents' liquor cabinet?

1156. When did you first learn to dance?

1157. Have you ever gone skinny dipping? When and with whom?

1158. What is the deepest level of grief that you have ever experienced? How long did it take you to get through the grieving process?

1159. What do you remember about turning age 16? What about turning age 18?

1160. Tell a story about your first pet. Was there a type of animal you wanted as a child but were unable to have? What other pets have you had throughout your life? Which, of all your pets, was your favorite? Have you ever had a pet that was more trouble than it was worth?

1161. Is there anything you have ever done that you are truly ashamed of?

1162. What did you normally do during summer vacation as a kid?

1163. Do you have a favorite airplane story? Has an airline ever lost your luggage? How did this affect your travel plans?

1164. When is the last time you had a get-together with family or friends? What did you do?

1165. When is the last time you had a block party with your neighbors?

1166. What interesting places have you traveled to? Where have you traveled outside your country?

1167. Can you recall a time when you just wanted to quit?

1168. Can you recall a time that you ran scared?

1169. Can you recall your most creative Halloween costume as a kid? Did you play any Halloween pranks? What friends do you remember sharing Halloween with?

1170. Have you ever gone parachuting, wind surfing, or for a balloon ride? Share your favorite story.

1171. Can you recall your proudest moment?

1172. Relate your favorite boating story.

1173. Can you recall a time that you took in a stray animal? What about an animal that you nurtured back to health?

1174. When was the last time you went skating?

1175. As a child, what were the first words you ever spoke?

1176. Did you ever feel violated by someone else? If yes, in what way?

1177. Did you have a secret hiding place as a child?

1178. Who were the singers or singing groups you enjoyed as a teenager?

1179. Who usually babysat you as a child? Can you recall any unusual babysitting experiences? Is there a babysitter you remember with a particular affection?

1180. Who were your favorite childhood TV personalities? What were your favorite TV programs to watch?

1181. Can you recall anyone reading to you as a child? Did you have a favorite bedtime story?

1182. Did you have any nicknames while growing up?

1183. Have you ever had a pen pal? If yes, who?

1184. What kinds of things were you praised for as a child? What kinds of things were you criticized for?

1185. Who, if anyone, spoiled you as a child?

1186. What kind of crazy things did you do at a slumber party or sleep-over as a youth?

1187. Are there people from your past whom you never want to see or hear from again? If yes, why?

1188. Have you ever had a dream that actually came true?

1189. Can you remember your first day of school?

1190. Did you ever wear braces?

1191. What were your favorite outside games and activities as a youth?

1192. Can you recall a time when you "got caught" doing something you shouldn't have?

1193. Has there ever been a time in your life that your mind was so cluttered and confused that you couldn't make a decision about what or which direction to take?

1194. Have you ever felt totally humiliated?

1195. Can you recall something cruel you did to someone as a kid? Can you recall something cruel someone else did to you as a kid?

1196. What was the worst illness you ever experienced?

1197. Are there certain times in your life that you feel you have misspent your energies?

1198. When did you feel the freedom and courage to move on?

1199. At what age did you sow your wild oats?

1200. When is the last time you did something completely unpredictable, spontaneous, and just a little bit crazy?

1201. What is the most important or best decision you ever made in your life?

1202. Do previous stages of your life embarrass you? If yes, in what way and for what reason? Is there anything from your past that you worry about catching up with you?

1203. What has been the most difficult transitional period of your life?

1204. Have you ever gone through a process of reassembling your identity?

1205. What has been your greatest life challenge?

1206. When was the last time you went the extra mile for the sole benefit of another person? When was the last time you remember someone else going the extra mile for you?

1207. What do you think you've paid too high a price for doing or having?

1208. Have you ever tried to bargain with God? What were the circumstances?

1209. Have you ever had a premonition? Explain.

1210. Can you recall a time that you felt like you failed? What do you think was the cause of your failure? What, if anything, did you learn from that experience?

1211. Have you ever had to sacrifice one thing for another?

1212. When and what were your first thoughts about God?

1213. Have you ever been in such serious trouble that you thought there would be no way out? What was the outcome?

1214. When has something you said gotten you into trouble?

1215. At what times in your life have you been placed in a position of leadership? How well did you lead?

1216. What is the one mistake that you made that cost you the most? What price did you pay?

1217. Can you recall a time that you believe God heard and answered your prayers?

1218. When and at what times have you felt emotionally exposed?

1219. Can you recall a time when you were particularly brave (not the illusion of appearing brave, but actually brave)?

1220. Were you ever lucky enough to have a mentor? What did he/she teach you about life?

1221. When and at what age did you find your niche in life?

1222. What religious training did you have as a child?

1223. When were you too rigid for your own good?

1224. Have you ever been baptized? Where and at what age?

1225. To what project do you remember giving your greatest personal level of dedication?

1226. Do you believe in miracles? Has anything ever happened in your life that you would consider a miracle?

1227. Have you ever been afraid to go after something or someone that you wanted? If yes, who or what? What were you afraid might happen if you did?

1228. What has life taught you?

1229. What is your birthdate? Where were you born and at what time? What is your most memorable birthday? What would be your favorite way to spend your birthday?

1230. Have you ever had a supernatural experience? If yes, explain.

1231. When did you step forward or take a real stand? Was it worth your energies? What was the final outcome?

1232. Were you ever voted to receive any special honors or awards?

1233. Have you ever been jealous over someone or something? Of whom or what were you jealous? Why do you think you felt this way?

1234. Have you ever felt lost?

1235. When did you succeed at something that you thought was impossible?

1236. Have you ever experienced mental telepathy?

1237. When was the last time you were bold in the face of intimidation? When was the last time you walked away a coward?

1238. Can you recall a time when you felt that you had a new beginning?

1239. When have you been in the right place at the right time? When have you been in the **wrong** place at the wrong time?

1240. What has been the most difficult lesson you have ever had to learn? If you could **erase** that experience, would you, or would you choose to **keep** the learning experience for the sole purpose of what it taught you?

1241. Did you ever have a light go off in your head and you knew the **exact** path to take?

1242. When was the last time you felt **real** passion for anything?

1243. When did you think you were right and then realized you were wrong?

1244. Can you recall a time when you regretted your actions? What would you have done differently?

1245. When is the last time you had to eat humble pie?

1246. Recall a time that you felt completely alone.

1247. Can you remember your last "do it yourself" project? How did it turn out?

1248. Can you recall a situation that hurt you deeply?

1249. What is the one thing you never thought would happen but did?

1250. What is something that you discovered but wished you hadn't? Have you ever seen something you wished you hadn't?

1251. Can you recall ever having to step out in blind faith?

1252. What was the **first** thing to kindle your passion towards life?

1253. Can you recall ever thinking your pain would never go away?

1254. When was the last time you heard the words "I love you"? When was the last time you told someone else you loved them?

1255. Who can make you laugh? And when was the last time you laughed so hard it hurt? Who were you with and what was the topic of your humor?

1256. Describe a situation when you realized you had made the mistake of your life.

1257. When is the last time you had butterflies in your stomach?

1258. Have there been times in your life when you stagnated? When and what do you feel caused this problem?

1259. Recall a time you felt the need to hide behind a mask? Explain why.

1260. When did you experience a victory?

1261. Can you recall the very lowest point of your life?

1262. Have you ever had your driver's license revoked? How many tickets have you gotten in your life? What were they for?

1263. Have you ever been attacked by anyone? Are you capable of protecting yourself if you were attacked? If yes, how?

1264. What were your favorite subjects in school? Were there any particular subjects that you struggled with in school? Did you ever cheat?

1265. Have you ever backed out of a situation at the last minute? When and why?

1266. Were you ever the underdog? When and what were the circumstances?

1267. Can you recall having a food, pillow, or water fight?

1268. Have you ever been shot, stabbed, or wounded in any way? Have you ever witnessed this happening to someone else?

1269. Can you recall a specific illness you suffered as a child?

1270. Can you tell a story about a time you played hooky from school?

1271. Have you ever gone to a class reunion? How did you feel about the event? What friend did you most enjoy being reunited with? Who or what surprised you the most?

1272. What was your most memorable trip taken by car?

1273. Recall a special experience you had at the fair, a carnival, or the circus. Who were you with and what did you enjoy the most?

1274. Did you ever have to wear someone else's hand-me-downs? If yes, how did you feel about having to do so?

1275. Have you ever won a contest? If yes, what was it for and what did you win?

1276. Can you recall the most special gift you received as a child?

1277. Recall your worst personal emergency. Have you ever helped someone in an emergency situation? If yes, explain.

1278. Have you ever been poor? Recall the times in your life that you were completely broke. What did you do to pull yourself out of that hole? What did you learn at such times?

1279. Have you ever been wrongly accused of something? If yes, how did that make you feel? Was the situation ever resolved?

1280. Did anyone close to you die when you were a child? How did you deal with this situation?

1281. When did you act so ugly in a situation that you were actually ashamed of yourself and your own behavior?

1282. Have you ever gone to night school to try to improve your education? If yes, what courses did you pursue?

1283. Have you ever shared a confidence with someone and later regretted doing so? When has someone betrayed a confidence you shared with him/her?

1284. Can you share a memory about something that happened on the way home from school as a youth? How did you get back and forth from school? If you walked, who do you remember walking home with?

1285. Have you ever had your feelings hurt over not being invited to something?

1286. What childhood bonds with someone other than family members do you have that run very deep?

1287. What do you recall about your years in elementary school? What about your friendships? Can you recall each one of your teachers' names and something about them, grades 1-6?

1288. Can you remember having your feelings hurt as a child? Who hurt them and what was it over?

1289. What fond memories do you have about going to the beach as a youth, a teenager, and an adult? In general, how do you feel about the beach?

1290. Did you go to your prom? What was prom night like for you, where did you go, and what did you do? Who besides your date shared the evening with you?

1291. Can you recall a project you worked on that had you known the exact amount of time, energy, and aggravation involved, you would never have had the courage to start?

1292. What is the hardest physical labor that you have ever done?

1293. Have you ever had an experience you couldn't believe was actually happening to you? If yes, what?

1294. Have you ever felt your energy blocked? If yes, what blocked it?

1295. When did you last feel like someone was ungrateful? When did you last feel like someone was very grateful?

1296. What is the most dangerous situation you have ever been in? When have you narrowly escaped from a dangerous situation? How did you escape?

1297. Have you ever done something that made you look or feel like a total fool?

1298. Looking back, can you ever remember being small or petty about a particular situation?

1299. Have you ever done something for all the wrong reasons? If yes, what?

1300. When has something been left unsaid that should have been talked through and understood?

1301. Have you ever felt a Holy presence? Have you ever felt an evil influence? If yes, explain.

1302. Has anything ever happened in your life that was beyond reasonable understanding— something that had no logical explanation? If yes, explain.

1303. Were you ever a Brownie, Girl Scout, Cub Scout or Boy Scout? Have you ever been a group leader?

1304. When was the last time you were able to completely forgive someone for a wrong committed against you? When do you feel like someone completely forgave you for a wrong you committed against him/her?

1305. When have you surrendered to someone or to a situation?

1306. Have you ever resisted change? If yes, explain.

1307. Go back to your junior high school years. Recall an incident that really sticks out in your mind.

1308. Did you and your high school friends have a favorite place to gather or hang out together?

1309. What project did you have to complete for home economics or shop class when you were in junior high? How did it turn out?

1310. Who do you remember as the class clown, the class bully, and the class brain?

1311. Have you ever done something to embarrass your family?

1312. How often did you go to the movies as a kid? How much did you pay to get in and whom did you usually go with?

1313. What is one thing you feel you missed out on as a kid?

1314. Do you have any blind date stories? Have you ever played matchmaker with someone? What was the outcome?

1315. Tell a story about your first true love. How old were you?

1316. How old were you when you had your first sexual experience? How would you describe the experience?

1317. Have you ever made love in the back seat of a car?

1318. Can you remember your first case of puppy love?

1319. Who was your high school sweetheart? How long did you go together? Do you know where he/she is and what they are doing with their life?

1320. Did you go parking when you were a teenager? If yes, when, where, and with whom?

1321. What is the secret of the mustard seed?

1322. How would you feel if the holiday season was celebrated with gifts from the heart instead of material gifts?

1323. How would it feel to reach the point of death, only to realize you had never really lived?

1324. If the statement is true that water seeks its own level, what would knowing your friends tell about you?

1325. What qualities do you think make a person lovable? Who do you know that has these qualities?

1326. What is a gift that lives on?

1327. How do you feel or what do you think when you see someone on the side of the road with a sign that says, "I will work for food"?

1328. What makes a holiday special for you?
- being with family
- holiday music
- special smells and foods
- holiday decorations
- holiday parties
- other

1329. Are you creative enough to develop an idea that could make a contribution to society? If yes, what?

1330. When have you stopped to help someone in need?

1331. What can't money buy for you?

1332. What are the most critical problems our nation faces?

1333. What is charisma? Who do you know with this quality?

1334. Is there any situation that you would like to get to the heart of?

1335. Can you do any impressions?

1336. How many hours a week do you watch TV? What kinds of programs do you enjoy watching? Do you feel television should be censored?

1337. If you had to leave this country, what other country would you choose to live in and why?

1338. Have you ever met someone you instantly disliked? If yes, why? What about someone you instantly liked? If yes, why?

1339. What do you serve for dinner on a special holiday?

1340. Do you think hell exists? What do you think will actually go on there? Do you believe in the Devil?

1341. What do you consider are the true riches of life?

1342. How do you think our universe came into existence?

1343. Is democracy the best form of government?

1344. Where or how can someone find happiness? Are you happy? If yes, what makes you happy?

1345. In what ways does society abuse the environment at the expense of the future generations?

1346. What is faith and how does it work?

1347. Can you give some ideas concerning the type of gift you would like to receive on your birthday or a special occasion?

1348. What changes would you make in our nation's educational system? How do you feel our system compares with other leading nations?

1349. Do you have great respect for any particular nationality? If yes, why?

1350. What will you be remembered for when you die? Who would you like to speak about you at your funeral?

1351. How often do you rent video tapes? What have been some of your all-time favorite films?

1352. What magazines would someone find in your home?

1353. When is it a good time to compromise?

1354. What things do you consider holy?

1355. Do you like to shop? How often and where? What kind of shopper are you?

1356. In case of a disaster, where would you seek shelter?

1357. How would winning the lottery change your life?

1358. What should the penalty be for habitual drunk drivers?

1359. How do you feel about gambling?

1360. How do you feel about Living Wills?

1361. What is evil? What is the most evil thought you have ever had? What has been your most evil action?

1362. Complete this sentence: If I could know the absolute truth about any one thing, it would be . . .

1363. If your state has a lottery, do you agree with the way your state spends proceeds?

1364. How do you feel about American land being bought by foreign countries?

1365. What political issues do you support and why?

1366. Is it possible to know God? Do you believe in the concept of a personal God?

1367. How do you think the different races came about?

1368. How patriotic are you? Would you serve your country in time of war? What if you did not agree with the issues being fought over?

1369. Is there anything that you see as becoming a potential problem? What could you do at this point to stop this problem from developing?

1370. Do you have a favorite place to go out for dinner? Where would you like to dine on a very special occasion?

1371. What does winning mean to you, being first or being your best?

1372. Who or what is the Holy Spirit?

1373. Who are your senators, state representatives, and Governor?

1374. When is the last time you sent or received a telegram? What did the telegram say?

1375. Whom do you know with a green thumb?

1376. Who is your favorite newscaster? Is it important to you to keep up with what's going on in the world? How often do you watch the news?

1377. Do you feel freedom of speech is carried too far by the news media or not far enough?

1378. Do you believe in eternal life, predestination, Karma, or reincarnation?

1379. Do you feel that the federal government has too much power, or not enough?

1380. What is your favorite wine?

1381. Do you attempt to stay informed about issues so that you can vote intelligently?

1382. Do you feel you have the right to complain about how your country is run if you fail to vote?

1383. Do you shop for sales?

1384. Do you go to garage sales? What was your all-time best bargain found at a garage sale?

1385. How often do you wash and wax your car? Is the type of car you drive important to you? If money were not an issue, what kind of car would you drive?

1386. Have you ever written a letter that you later regretted sending?

1387. Where can truth be found?

1388. How has the women's liberation movement changed things in our society?

1389. How do you see our country 20 years from now?

1390. Could you detect a con man? Have you ever been the victim of a con man/woman? Has anyone ever cleverly deceived or cheated you? If yes, explain.

1391. Why do you think the crime rate is so high in our country?

1392. When and how do you think the world will end?

1393. Do you enjoy traveling? Is there a certain place you have always wanted to visit? How do you prepare for a trip?

1394. What do you think it would be like to be a different race and color?

1395. You enter your car and are accosted by a stranger who instructs you to drive to a secluded area. What do you do?

1396. If you had the opportunity to visit another planet with alien beings to learn about their world, would you go? What if you could never return?

1397. In your opinion, who do you think Jesus Christ was and what do you think was His message?

1398. What problems will children born in the 1990s encounter in their future?

1399. How would you feel if low-income housing or a nuclear power plant were built close to your home?

1400. How do you respond when someone tells a political, ethnic, or dirty joke?

1401. In your opinion, what makes someone a winner?

1402. What percentage of wealthy people do you believe are happy and content?

1403. Have you ever broken a prized possession? What is your most prized material possession?

1404. Have you ever sued someone or been sued? If yes, for what reason?

1405. What would be your idea of a great invention?

1406. Are there such things as spiritual laws that govern life?

1407. If you could have been born during another period in history, when would it be and why?

1408. What is your favorite fast food restaurant?

1409. A stranger comes to your door and appears to be hurt. Will you let him in?

1410. How many hours a day would you be willing to work to accomplish a worthwhile project?

1411. What are your feelings when you pass a homeless person on the street? Do you ever give him/her money?

1412. What is your favorite late night snack?

1413. What are your views on the present tax laws?

1414. If you had to split your life up like a pie, who or what would get the biggest slice (family, work, career, education, etc.)?

1415. How do you like to celebrate New Year's Eve? What did you do last New Year's Eve?

1416. Is there a book that has a special meaning for you?

1417. Is there a ticket to heaven? Or hell?

1418. How do you respond when someone gives you a gift you don't like?

1419. In the middle of the night you hear someone in your house. How do you respond?

1420. How conscientious are you when it comes to conserving energy? What about those you live with?

1421. How do you feel about the relationship between the United States and the Soviet Union?

1422. If you are over age 30, where were you when President John F. Kennedy was killed?

1423. What is your favorite sport? How often do you view sports on TV?

1424. If you could blink your eyes and something would suddenly disappear or appear, what would that be?

1425. Who would you consider a wise person?

1426. Do you believe in heaven? If so, what do you think people will actually do there?

1427. What anxieties do you have around the holidays?

1428. What are your plans when you retire?

1429. Have you ever gone through a natural disaster? When and where was it, and how were you affected?

1430. Tell your favorite joke.

1431. What are your thoughts and opinions on our present welfare system?

1432. How often do you go out to see a movie?

1433. Would you pay a good deal of money for a piece of art?

1434. Do you think women should be drafted into the Armed Forces for combat duty?

1435. If you believe in God, do you think He has a purpose for each person?

1436. What is your political affiliation?

1437. At the point of death what do you think actually happens? If you believe in an afterlife, what do you think are the sequence of events that take place as a soul jorneys from this world to the next?

1438. How would you feel if someone gave you a surprise party? How do you feel when someone sings "Happy Birthday" to you in a restaurant?

1439. What do you consider nature's most beautiful gift to mankind? When was the last time you noticed and enjoyed the beauty of nature?

1440. Do you believe that virtues and vices survive death?

1441. How do you believe mankind, nature, and the animals came into existence?

1442. You run out of gas in a completely isolated area at 3:00 a.m. A strange-looking character stops to help you. What do you do?

1443. Do you believe prayer can bring answers to difficult problems in life?

1444. Do you believe in fate, chance, or destiny?

1445. Do you give your opinion when it isn't solicited? Who gives you their opinion whether you want it or not?

1446. How is the quest for happiness sometimes perverted?

1447. Relate your worst animal training story.

1448. Do you believe there is an unseen spiritual world that surrounds us?

1449. What would you need to consider yourself rich?

1450. Who really determines what happens in this country?

1451. What is the soul of a person?

1452. What are the best things in life?

1453. If you were given a part to play in a movie, what part would that be?

1454. What have you never understood?

1455. Do you attend church or synagogue?

1456. Do you enjoy having fresh cut flowers in your home? What are some of your favorite flowers?

1457. Would you ever consider hiring a surrogate mother if you were unable to have children?

1458. If you were a guest on a talk show, what subject would you feel most qualified to discuss?

1459. If you were to write a book, what would the subject and title be?

1460. How do you feel about the President of the United States of America? Who do you think would make a great next president?

1461. What was the most startling thing that happened to you in the middle of the night?

1462. What do you like in a salad? What is your favorite dressing? What is your favorite kind of salad?

1463. How do you like your
   • pizza
   • coffee
   • eggs
   • meat cooked?

1464. What do you think is the best way to help the poor and homeless?

1465. Do you celebrate Easter? If so, how?

1466. What useful household hint could you share with someone?

1467. What do you think everyone is looking for in life?

1468. How do you contribute to your country?

1469. What do you think the human mind is really capable of? If you used even 50% of your brain power, what do you think you could accomplish? What new dimensions could you tap into?

1470. When did you stay longer than you should have?

1471. What do you usually think about when you drive in your car?

1472. What do you think really exists beyond the stars?

1473. There is true success and the illusion of success. How can you distinguish between the two?

1474. What would be your ideal vacation?

1475. What is your favorite holiday and why?

1476. How do you feel about receiving visitors when you're sick in the hospital or at home?

1477. Do you believe it is possible for the mind to regenerate and heal the body?

1478. What makes one person succeed in spite of major obstacles and another fail having been given every possible opportunity to succeed?

1479. Can you recall your most inspirational experience?

1480. Do you believe astrology has any credence?

1481. How do you feel when someone forgets your birthday? What do you do when you have forgotten someone on a very special occasion?

1482. What recent news event have you followed very carefully?

1483. What is the most desirable and admirable characteristic to possess?

1484. Would you like a peek into the supernatural world? If yes, what do you think you would see?

1485. If you dreamed that your plane crashed the night before you were to take a trip, what would you do?

1486. If someone could go though your wallet or purse, what would they find out about you? What if they could go through your dresser?

1487. What is your idea of a well-dressed man? How about a well-dressed woman?

1488. If you had to be stranded on a desert island for one year with someone other than a family member, whom would you choose?

1489. Complete this sentence: I think a new law should be written to . . .

1490. What do you think are the most important qualities necessary to achieve excellence at a given task?

1491. What support, if any, should the United States give to other countries?

1492. What do you consider true genius?

1493. When was your timing critical in the outcome of a situation?

1494. What would you do if someone tried to blackmail you?

1495. What one thing do you want to do or see before you die?

1496. What famous person in history would you have liked to know on a personal level?

1497. Can you see yourself as homeless? If you lost your job and home, and had no family or friends, what would you do?

1498. How do you feel and what do you say when someone butts in front of you when you're waiting in line?

1499. How is your health at this particular point in your life?

1500. What is your very favorite time of the year and why?

1501. If you could keep the wisdom and learning that you gained from life and return to any age in your life, what age would that be?

1502. Complete this sentence: My favorite time of day is . . . Explain why.

1503. Have you ever seen something that you wish you hadn't?

1504. Share a story about being locked out of your house, car, or office.

1505. Have you ever had any broken bones? If yes, when and what happened?

1506. Men - would you invest in a hairpiece if you were going bald? Would you consider a hair transplant?

1507. What can you create or design with your hands?

1508. Have you ever chased after something and when you got it, realized it was not what you wanted to begin with?

1509. Would you be willing to give up sex for life if you were guaranteed perfect mental, physical, and emotional health until you were 90 (at that point, you would die in your sleep).

1510. Have you ever asked someone for an honest opinion and then had your feelings hurt when he/she gave it to you?

1511. Do you ever say things you do not mean? If yes, when and for what reason?

1512. Who do you know that is not a straight shooter? Who do you know who **is** a straight shooter?

1513. In what ways have your attitudes, ideas, and values changed with age?

1514. Would you be willing to live in total seclusion for one year if you could emerge with great wisdom that would affect the rest of your life?

1515. Do you get along better with men or women? Why?

1516. If you needed critical information and you had a friend who could get this information for you, but it would jeopardize this person's job, would you still ask your friend to obtain the information anyway?

1517. If you could choose one thing at which you could become highly successful, what would that be?

1518. What would you do if you saw an injured animal on the side of the road?

1519. Do you think you live a life more satisfying or less satisfying than other people's?

1520. Can you recall a time that a special occasion turned into a total disaster?

1521. How would you feel if you were handicapped? Would it bother you to be seen as a handicapped person?

1522. Have you had any opportunity slip through your fingers?

1523. What would you give your eyeteeth for?

1524. Can you recall a time when you felt that you did not get your money's worth?

1525. Do you think there still exists a double standard between men and women? If yes, why and what is the rationale behind this?

1526. How do you handle pushy, crude, rude or difficult people?

1527. What would happen if we actually made contact with beings from outer space? How do you think they view our world and the way we live?

1528. Do you follow through or are you all talk and no action?

1529. When do you think life really began for you?

1530. What do you think about mercy killing?

1531. Do you have anything unique or something you are proud of hanging on the walls in your home or office?

1532. Is there such a thing as an inner guide?

1533. Have you ever or do you know anyone who has experienced a supernatural healing? If yes, explain.

1534. What unexplored dimensions would you like to investigate?

1535. What gives you great pleasure to watch?

1536. Do you believe it is possible to tap into energy outside of yourself?

1537. How good are your survival skills and instincts? Could you survive in the wilderness? If yes, how and for what length of time?

1538. Is there anything you feel you're too old to do?

1539. How clean is your home and how clean are you as a person?

1540. Whose home besides your own do you feel at home in ?

1541. Do you contribute to any charities?

1542. When is the last time you sang or told ghost stories around a bonfire with family or friends? Who were you with?

1543. What would you consider a truly great wonder?

1544. Complete this sentence: My future looks. . .

1545. What is at the center of the universe?

1546. Who are your favorite TV personalities?

1547. Complete this sentence: I'd like to become the best at . . .

1548. Have you ever felt that someone was more concerned with what you had than who you were? If yes, who?

1549. Who in your neighborhood could use your help?

1550. Who is your favorite comedian?

1551. Do you ever misuse your energy by putting on a performance for the sake of other people? Can you recall a time that you did this?

1552. Do you save coupons and shop for bargains or are you an impulsive shopper?

1553. Have you ever had to pay for someone else's mistakes? If yes, what were the circumstances?

1554. Do you play a sport? If yes, what has been your all-time best score?

1555. Have you ever had to call the police? If yes, what for?

1556. Complete this sentence: I felt what I said was misunderstood the time . . .

1557. In your opinion, what would be a good way to straighten out the economy and the country?

1558. Men - If you found out that a child you thought was yours for 16 years actually belonged to another man, what would you do?

1559. Has your home, office, or car ever been broken into? If yes, what was stolen and were the perpetrators caught?

1560. Do you believe there are other intelligent life forms in our universe? If yes, what do you think they are like? Do you think we will have contact with other beings in our lifetime?

1561. If the statement is true that a man reaps exactly what he has sown, nothing more, nothing less, then what do you have to look forward to?

1562. Would you employ someone like yourself? Why or why not?

1563. How much effort and dedication do you put into your present job?

1564. What are your greatest assets when it comes to business smarts?

1565. Would you report a co-worker who was stealing from your company?

1566. Do you ever have the desire to change career fields? What new field would you pursue?

1567. What abilities and special talents do you offer your employer?

1568. Has your job ever interfered with your family life?

1569. What level of success do you want to obtain in your career?

1570. If you knew that a neighbor was abusing her children, what would you do?

1571. The bank teller machine gives you $10,000 instead of $10.00. What will you do?

1572. You are offered a great buy on a beautiful piece of jewelry. You suspect it is stolen. Would you still buy it?

1573. While shopping for a winter coat, you notice that the one you like is priced incorrectly (in your favor). Would you tell the clerk?

1574. Have you ever had an idea that you thought could make you a lot of money?

1575. If you got divorced, how would you split up your estate?

1576. Do you have a financial plan for the future?

1577. How much money do you spend on entertainment each month?

1578. What do you feel is the wisest way to invest money?

1579. Have you ever been poor? When and to what degree?

1580. If your mate wanted to quit his/her job and invest your entire savings in a new business venture, would you support him/her?

1581. Do you feel that having a nest egg is important?

1582. Has there ever been a time that you have felt someone took advantage of you? Have you ever taken advantage of someone else?

1583. What would you do if you were convicted of a crime you did not commit and were sentenced to life in prison?

1584. Have you ever borrowed money and not returned it? If yes, how did you justify not returning it? Has anyone ever borrowed money from you and not returned it? If yes, did it hurt your relationship with that person?

1585. What is the greatest injustice you have ever experienced or witnessed?

1586. If you had a major illness three years ago and were applying for health insurance, would you be honest about your past illness?

1587. Can you come up with a solution to help decrease the problem of world hunger?

1588. What are your views on the gun laws in our country?

1589. In what ways do you waste money?

1590. When you go out to dinner with friends, how do you handle the check?

1591. Have you ever knowingly made a false promise?

1592. What would you do if you did not have enough money to pay your rent and you found a wallet containing $3,000?

1593. In what ways do you personally try to protect our environment? How do you feel when you see someone throw trash out the window?

1594. Do you lie? What about white lies? Is there ever a time that telling a lie is appropriate? What is the most whopping lie you have ever told?

1595. Do you believe that all things that go around, come around?

1596. What do you think about a new machine that allows terminally ill patients to end their suffering?

1597. Have you ever lied about your age?

1598. Would you lend money to a friend, business associate, or family member?

1599. How would you react if your mate had a secret bank account? Would you ever consider having a secret bank account?

1600. How would you feel if your mate donated money to a cause that you disagreed with?

1601. Do you have any money or material possessions that you feel belong to you and are not jointly owned?

1602. Give a history of your spending habits.

1603. Is there anything really holding you back from doing what you want?

1604. Do you have an all-time favorite boss? Who? Why? What about your all-time worst boss? Who? Why?

1605. When is the last time you got a raise or a promotion? What was your most memorable promotion?

1606. What are other things you could do to make a living?

1607. Have you ever been a workaholic? If so, are you still a workaholic?

1608. As a teenager, what were some of the careers you considered?

1609. You receive your credit card bill. You notice that a $500.00 purchase does not appear. Will you notify the credit card company?

1610. What crimes, if any, have you committed?

1611. How honest are you? Who is the most honest person you know?

1612. Would you intervene if you witnessed an assault?

1613. Have you ever had a bad or questionable reputation?

1614. How do you feel about the legal system in the United States?

1615. What should we do with the severely retarded people in our society? What about the criminally insane?

1616. You accidentally back into someone else's car. There are no witnesses. Do you leave your name and phone number?

1617. Do you have a hobby that you could turn into a small business for additional income?

1618. What are some of the financial sacrifices you have made in the past?

1619. Do you have a financial goal that you share with your partner?

1620. What are your past and present debts?

1621. How large does a purchase need to be before you discuss it with your mate?

1622. Do you have a difficult time managing money? Have you ever?

1623. How could you earn money at home?

1624. Are you conservative with credit card spending or do you charge to the limit?

1625. Your mate loves his/her job but could make a great deal more money doing something else. The family needs the additional income. Would you ask him/her to change careers?

1626. How important is your need for affirmation from your boss?

1627. Have you ever been fired from a job? What were the circumstances?

1628. What career goal would you like to achieve over the next year?

1629. Can you recall a co-worker you got along with very well? What about one you didn't get along with?

1630. You work for a family-owned business and realize that one of the family members has been embezzling money. What would you do?

1631. Would you lie in court to keep your closest friend, a family member, or business associate from going to jail?

1632. A family member you love dearly commits a serious crime. The judge gives you the responsibility of choosing the punishment. How do you respond?

1633. You work for a surgeon who you come to realize has a heavy drug or drinking problem. What do you do?

1634. Would you give a letter of recommendation to an employee you fired? The employee is a single mother with five children.

1635. Would you ever use a Watts line at work to make personal calls?

1636. How do you feel about wearing animal fur?

1637. Would you report someone who was receiving social security benefits illegally?

1638. Have you ever held a job that was beneath your abilities? What about one that was beyond your abilities?

1639. How should the financial responsibility be handled in your household?

1640. Is there a secret to prosperity?

1641. What is the total average of all your monthly bills?

1642. Do you budget your money?

1643. How much did you spend last year on car repairs and maintenance?

1644. How important is it to you to have a will? Do you feel your will is in order? When was the last time you updated your will?

1645. Would you ever consider a joint investment with a friend, family member, or business associate?

1646. Your boss humiliates you in front of a client. How do you respond?

1647. How would you handle a fellow employee with whom you cannot get along?

1648. Would you be willing to relocate for your mate? What if you had the job of your dreams?

1649. What is the longest period of time that you were unemployed?

1650. What different types of jobs have you had in your life?

1651. Does your mate support your chosen career?

1652. Do you believe the end justifies the means?

1653. Have you ever done something that you consider truly sinful?

1654. Do you respect the dignity of all people? Are there any people you treat in a disrespectful manner? If yes, why?

1655. Is there anything that you have ever done that you regret?

1656. Have you ever cheated on an exam?

1657. Have you ever used a fake I.D.?

1658. How do you feel about abortion?

1659. Are you working at a job you like? If not, why are you there?

1660. Have you ever worked for an incompetent boss?

1661. What is your favorite way to spend mad money?

1662. Would it bother you if your mate had a higher income than you?

1663. When you give a donation, is it ever anonymous?

1664. Do you pay child support or alimony?

1665. Is there a particular bill you hate to pay?

1666. Have you ever taken out a bank loan?

1667. Have you ever stopped payment on a check? Why?

1668. What is a good way to teach children how to handle money?

1669. Do you save coupons?

1670. Did you ever get a job based on who you knew rather than what you knew?

1671. Did you choose your job based on what best suited you in terms of personality, education, and desire?

1672. What is the last book you read that helped you with your business?

1673. Do you feel it is possible to be completely honest in business?

1674. Your uncle bought a restaurant with illegal drug money. Would you eat there?

1675. Would you convict a woman for killing her husband if there was proof of physical and emotional abuse?

1676. Have you ever cheated on your income taxes? If yes, to what extent?

1677. You witness a robbery. You notice the robber is your younger brother. Will you turn him in?

1678. Have you ever done something illegal?

1679. What would you do if you caught an employee you were very fond of stealing from you or from the company?

1680. What makes a good boss? Would you make a good boss?

1681. How would you earn extra money if you needed it?

1682. What is your greatest weakness when it comes to spending money?

1683. How important is financial security to you?

1684. What lessons have you learned in times of financial struggle?

1685. How much do you average in medical expenses each year? Do you have any medical debts?

1686. Have you ever cheated your employer by using his/her time to work on a personal project?

1687. What is your biggest money problem?

1688. Who pays the bills in your household?

1689. How much of what you earn do you consider is family funds and how much do you feel is yours to spend as you choose?

1690. How and why did you choose the job in which you are presently employed?

1691. If you had to write an advertisement to sell yourself to a new boss, what would the ad say?

1692. Could you ever be in business with your family?

1693. Can you recall a time when you worked on something that took true teamwork?

1694. Have you ever read someone's mail or listened in on someone's private conversation?

1695. What are your views on capital punishment? Could you ever actually push the button?

1696. Have you ever torn a recipe out of a magazine at your doctor's or dentist's office?

1697. Would you recommend a friend for a position in your company? She has been unemployed for six months and has a heavy drinking problem.

1698. How do you feel about people living together before they get married?

1699. How do you feel about accepting an expensive gift from someone?

1700. Do you feel there should be a mandatory age for retirement?

1701. How well do you work under pressure?

1702. Would you help a family member end his/her life if he/she were terminally ill?

1703. Would you help your 16-year-old daughter obtain birth control pills if she asked for your assistance?

1704. Is there any amount of money that would entice you to leave your country, friends, and family?

1705. If a friend's child was hurt in your home, would you offer to pay the medical bills?

1706. If you were fired tomorrow, what would you do?

1707. How would you feel about signing a prenuptial agreement?

1708. Do you play the lottery?

1709. Have you ever worried about where tomorrow's bread would come from?

1710. If you were to inherit money, would you consider it yours, or would you consider it joint funds with your spouse?

1711. Would you ever date your boss or someone with whom you work? How about someone who works for you?

1712. When was the last time you gave a hundred percent of what you had to give at work?

1713. Women - Have you ever had an abortion? How about a miscarriage? If so, what were the circumstances?

1714. What should the penalty be for rape?

1715. Have you ever been so angry with someone that you actually considered killing them?

1716. What should the penalty be for sexual abuse to children?

1717. What is your personal code of ethics?

1718. What should the penalty be for someone selling drugs? What about someone selling drugs to children?

1719. Would you contact the cable company if you were receiving free cable?

1720. Have you ever compromised your integrity? When did you fail to live by and follow your own true convictions?

1721. What percentage of your income do you save?

1722. Are you or have you ever been so engrossed in making a living that you neglect the emotional needs of your family?

1723. Can you recall a time you let a business opportunity slip through your fingers?

1724. Would you ever return something to a store that you already used?

1725. If someone were a guest in your home and you realized that he/she had stolen from you, what would you do? This is someone you have great affection for.

1726. If your mate became terminally ill, could you handle the financial and business responsibility of the family?

1727. What investment have you mad that has really paid off?

1728. How much money per year do you think you are worth? Explain why.

1729. How much importance do you place on someone's position or title? How much importance do you place on your own position or title?

1730. What, if anything, has dedication to your career cost you in human relationships? Is it necessary to make personal sacrifices in order to succeed?

1731. Have you ever failed at a professional endeavor? Why do you think you failed?

1732. Would you ever postpone marriage or having children for the sake of a well-established career?

1733. If you were a salesperson, could you sell a product you did not believe in? What if you really needed the income?

1734. How do you think the Ted Bundys of the world developed?

1735. How heavily do you rely on your gut instincts when it comes to making important business decisions?

1736. If you were independently wealthy, would you want to continue to work? If yes, would you continue to work in your present line of work whether you were being paid or not?

1737. What would you do if someone murdered a close family member and they were acquitted because of a technicality?

1738. If you had inherited one million dollars at age 18 how different would your life have been? Would it have helped or hindered your growth as a person?

1739. Should the father of an unborn child have any rights concerning the abortion of his unborn offspring?

1740. Would you continue to work at a job you hated if the monetary rewards were great?

1741. What do you think of any individual who acquires great wealth and position through cunning wit and intelligence but also through very deceptive measures?

1742. How do you feel about laboratory experiments that are done on live animals?

1743. A relative has taken care of your aging parents for several years. Would you resent that relative's getting part or all of your entire inheritance when your parents die?

1744. Would you ever work for a company that produced a product harmful to people (e.g., liquor company, cigarette company, nuclear power plant)?

1745. If you felt you were underpaid, would you still give your best to your employer?

1746. Would there be any price that would convince you to do something you thought was wrong? What if you had lost your job and were faced with losing your home?

1747. Would you visit a parent or grandparent in a nursing home whether they knew you were there or not?

1748. Would you give mouth to mouth resuscitation to a person who lives on the street?

1749. If your 16-year-old son got his girlfriend pregnant, how would you counsel him? If your 16-year-old daughter got pregnant, how would you counsel her?

1750. Would you ever read a file that had confidential information about you in it?

1751. If your teenager shared a strict confidence concerning your best friend's child, would you keep your mouth shut? It is a serious problem.

1752. A friend of yours has been implicated in a very serious crime; the evidence is very strong against her. Will this affect your relationship?

1753. Would you ever provide an alibi for a friend or family member?

1754. If your boss asked you to do jobs that are not work related, what would you tell him or her?

1755. How do you think criminals should be treated and disciplined in this country?

1756. Your best friends are getting divorced. One of them requested that you testify on his/her behalf in a child custody battle. What do you do?

1757. If someone borrowed money and did not pay it back, would you ask for the money?

1758. Can you recall a job interview that you were very nervous about?

1759. Would you lie for a friend who needed a false confirmation on earnings?

1760. How loyal are you to your employer? Do you have greater loyalty to your employer than your family? How loyal would your employer be if you became very ill?

1761. How would you feel if your parents left their entire estate to a charity, a good friend, or their church?

1762. Have you ever cleverly omitted half of the truth to change the meaning of a story?

1763. If you were selling your car, would you be completely honest about any and all past problems the car has had?

1764. Have you ever strongly attracted to your boss or someone you worked with? If yes, who?

1765. You are injured on the job due to your own carelessness; will you sue your employer?

1766. Have you ever had someone promoted over you and then were assigned to teach them their job?

1767. How do you feel about your boss? What about the people you work with?

1768. How honest, fair, and ethical are you when it comes to business dealings?

1769. You are independently wealthy and now your sole purpose and only job each day is to develop an idea, create a product, or provide a service that will enhance the lives and well-being of your fellow human beings. Where will you begin?

1770. Have you ever been self-employed? Have you ever considered starting your own business?

1771. Does your life work in some way bring something beneficial to others?

1772. Tell a story about a time you made a major blunder or mistake at work. What were the consequences?

1773. Have you or would you ever be willing to put your love life on hold so you could accomplish other worthwhile goals? If yes, for what period of time?

1774. If your earnings were a true reflection of your contribution, what kind of salary would you make?

1775. Tell a story about a sale or business deal you let slip through your fingers.

1776. Would you work for a boss who was dishonest, deceptive, and totally immoral if he were willing to pay you whatever you wanted (no limit)?

1777. How did you feel about this book? Your comments and honest feedback are important to us. Do you have any questions that you feel are valuable and should be included in our next printing? If yes, please write to us.

Send your comments to:

Character Builders
Aloma Business Center
6922 Aloma Avenue
Winter Park, FL 32792

COMMENTS

COMMENTS

COMMENTS

_____
_____
_____
_____
_____
_____
_____
_____
_____
_____
_____
_____
_____
_____
_____
_____
_____
_____
_____
_____
_____
_____
_____
_____
_____
_____
_____
_____

COMMENTS

COMMENTS

COMMENTS

COMMENTS

_____

_____

_____

_____

_____

_____

_____

_____

_____

_____

_____

_____

_____

_____

_____

_____

_____

_____

_____

_____

_____

_____

_____

_____

_____

_____

_____

_____

_____

COMMENTS

_____

_____

_____

_____

_____

_____

_____

_____

_____

_____

_____

_____

_____

_____

_____

_____

_____

_____

_____

_____

_____

_____

_____

_____

_____

_____

_____

_____

_____

_____

_____

COMMENTS

COMMENTS

COMMENTS

_____

_____

_____

_____

_____

_____

_____

_____

_____

_____

_____

_____

_____

_____

_____

_____

_____

_____

_____

_____

_____

_____

_____

_____

_____

_____

COMMENTS

COMMENTS

_____

_____

_____

_____

_____

_____

_____

_____

_____

_____

_____

_____

_____

_____

_____

_____

_____

_____

_____

_____

_____

_____

_____

_____

_____

_____

_____

_____

_____

COMMENTS

COMMENTS

_____

_____

_____

_____

_____

_____

_____

_____

_____

_____

_____

_____

_____

_____

_____

_____

_____

_____

_____

_____

_____

_____

_____

_____

_____

_____

_____

_____

COMMENTS

_____

_____

_____

_____

_____

_____

_____

_____

_____

_____

_____

_____

_____

_____

_____

_____

_____

_____

_____

_____

_____

_____

_____

_____

_____

_____

_____

_____

_____

_____

_____

COMMENTS

_____
_____
_____
_____
_____
_____
_____
_____
_____
_____
_____
_____
_____
_____
_____
_____
_____
_____
_____
_____
_____
_____
_____
_____
_____
_____
_____
_____
_____
_____
_____

COMMENTS

COMMENTS

_____

_____

_____

_____

_____

_____

_____

_____

_____

_____

_____

_____

_____

_____

_____

_____

_____

_____

_____

_____

_____

_____

_____

_____

_____

_____

_____

_____

_____

COMMENTS

COMMENTS

COMMENTS

COMMENTS

COMMENTS

COMMENTS

COMMENTS

_____

_____

_____

_____

_____

_____

_____

_____

_____

_____

_____

_____

_____

_____

_____

_____

_____

_____

_____

_____

_____

_____

_____

_____

_____

_____

_____

_____

_____

COMMENTS

_____
_____
_____
_____
_____
_____
_____
_____
_____
_____
_____
_____
_____
_____
_____
_____
_____
_____
_____
_____
_____
_____
_____
_____
_____
_____
_____
_____
_____

COMMENTS